moment and even more vital than when initially conceived. . . . Hayes has a particular talent for examining rather unflinchingly our national ills." —Matthew Pulver, *Salon*

"A major book, vital for our survival as a nation."
—Charles R. Larson, *CounterPunch*

"*A Colony in a Nation* reminds us that fear of the other, when weaponized and mechanized by the state, usually makes things worse. That's a lesson Americans of every color would do well to remember." —Eric Liu, *Washington Post*

"A thorough exploration of how the 'tough on crime' ideology leaves poor isolated minority populations living under a different set of laws." —Patrick Sauer, *Esquire*

"[Hayes] examines police tactics, drug policies, mass incarceration, and politics to highlight how blacks and whites, the poor and affluent have been treated differently by law enforcement." —WHYY

"[An] historic view of the concept of law and order in the United States." —Susan Whitehall, *Detroit News*

"Provocative . . . thought-provoking . . . persuasive."
—Thomas Chatterton Williams, *Bookforum*

Praise for

A COLONY IN A NATION

An Amazon Book of the Month (History), March 2017
New York Times Bestseller
New York Times Book Review Editors' Choice

"*A Colony in a Nation* is a highly original analysis of America's arbitrary and erratic criminal justice system. Indeed, by Hayes's lights, the system is not erratic at all—it treats one group of Americans as citizens, and another as the colonized. This is an essential and groundbreaking text in the effort to understand how American criminal justice went so badly awry."   —Ta-Nehisi Coates, author of
Between the World and Me

"Terrific and really important."   —Rebecca Traister

"A timely and impassioned argument for social justice."
          —*Kirkus Reviews*

"This readable and thoughtful work will appeal to readers interested in civil rights and criminal justice, and is especially insightful."   —William D. Pederson,
Library Journal (starred review)

"Writing with clarity, intelligence, and compassion, Hayes deftly illuminates the complex state of affairs that has evolved since the 1960s civil rights protests, and resulted in the current backlash." —*Booklist*

"Important, persuasive. . . . [*A Colony in a Nation*] can help Americans begin to heal." —*Publishers Weekly*

"Chris Hayes' ominous account of what's ailing America . . . [offers a] rare view into a wide racial and class cross-section of society." —Ryan Cooper, *The Week*

"An up-to-date (and masterfully interwoven) blend of statistics, history, and analysis." —Peter C. Baker, *Pacific Standard*

"Hayes is a forceful and eloquent writer. . . . He offers a clear and useful framework for understanding the current dysfunctions of American society. It's a brilliant diagnosis, [and] more urgent than ever." —Nick Romeo, *Christian Science Monitor*

"Hayes doesn't shy away from exposing bias where he finds it, which makes this passionate and well-researched account a compelling entry in the growing literature of social injustice." —Geoff McKenzie, *O, The Oprah Magazine*

"With perhaps the first significant theorization on race of the Trump era, Hayes delivers a book as dark and dire as the

ALSO BY CHRIS HAYES

Twilight of the Elites

CHRIS HAYES

A COLONY IN A NATION

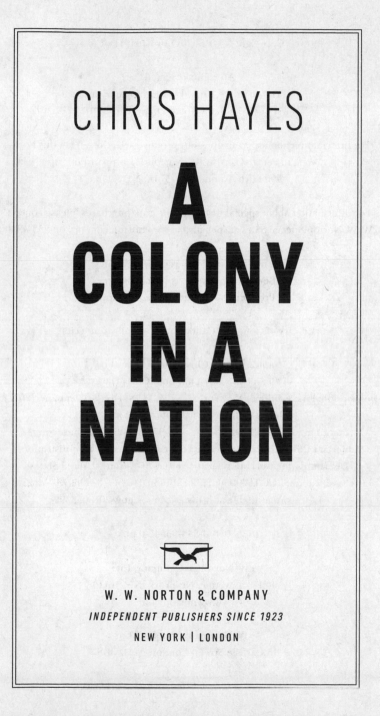

W. W. NORTON & COMPANY

INDEPENDENT PUBLISHERS SINCE 1923

NEW YORK | LONDON

For information about permission to reproduce selections from this book,
write to Permissions, W. W. Norton & Company, Inc.,
500 Fifth Avenue, New York, NY 10110

For information about special discounts for bulk purchases, please contact
W. W. Norton Special Sales at specialsales@wwnorton.com or 800-233-4830

Manufacturing by Berryville Graphics
Book design by Chris Welch Design
Production manager: Julia Druskin

Library of Congress Cataloging-in-Publication Data

Names: Hayes, Christopher L., author.
Title: A colony in a nation / Chris Hayes.
Description: First Edition. | New York, NY : W. W. Norton & Company, [2017] |
Includes bibliographical references and index.
Identifiers: LCCN 2016053392 | ISBN 9780393254228 (hardcover)
Subjects: LCSH: African Americans in criminal justice administration. |
Discrimination in criminal justice administration—United States.
Classification: LCC HV9950 .H396 2017 | DDC 364.3/496073—dc23
LC record available at https://lccn.loc.gov/2016053392

ISBN 978-0-393-35542-0 pbk

W. W. Norton & Company, Inc.
500 Fifth Avenue, New York, N.Y. 10110
www.wwnorton.com

W. W. Norton & Company Ltd.
15 Carlisle Street, London W1D 3BS

1 2 3 4 5 6 7 8 9 0

TO KATE, MY SOUL.

CONTENTS

A
COLONY
IN A
NATION

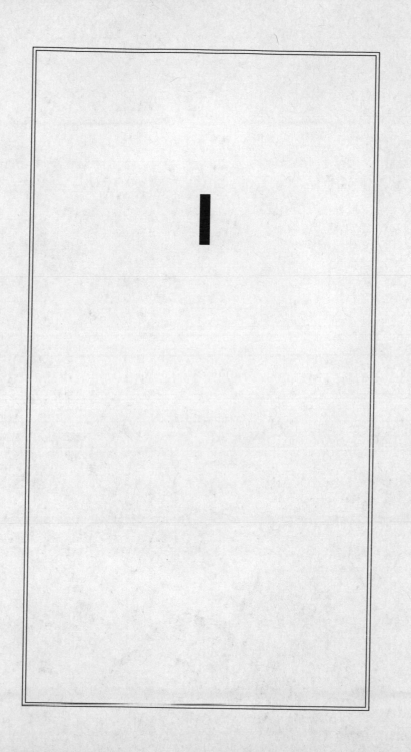

I

When was the last time you called the cops?

I'll go first.

It was a few years ago. I heard a couple arguing loudly on the street outside my apartment. "Arguing" probably undersells it—he was screaming as he leaned over her, his voice punching her ears: *"How stupid are you!?! What were you even thinking!?!"* and so forth. The argument echoed through the dark in the leafy, affluent neighborhood I live in. Here we are unused to street noise of that particular type. I listened for a few minutes, and then some part of me thought, *I know how this ends.* So I dialed 911 and told the dispatcher what I was hearing. A few minutes later, from the dark of my apartment, I peeked out the window and saw the swirling blue light of a police cruiser. The car pulled over, and two cops approached the couple. I stopped watching and went to bed. Mission accomplished.

But whatever happened to that couple? To that woman?

I have no idea. I thought at that moment, and would still like to think, that I called the cops because I was trying to protect her from a conflict that was likely to end in violence. But maybe I just wanted peace and quiet restored to my peaceful and quiet neighborhood. As much as I told myself in that moment that I was calling the cops on her behalf, I have no idea if she would've wanted me to make that call, or if it made her life any better. For all I know, the encounter with the police only made him angrier, and she bore the brunt of that anger in their apartment, hours later.

Whatever became of her, one thing is clear to me in retrospect. At the moment I called the police, I could not have told you what law was being broken, what crime was being committed. I dialed that number not to enforce the law but to restore order.

There are fundamentally two ways you can experience the police in America: as the people you call when there's a problem, the nice man in uniform who pats a toddler's head and has an easy smile for the old lady as she buys her coffee. For others, the police are the people who are called on them. They are the ominous knock on the door, the sudden flashlight in the face, the barked orders. Depending on who you are, the sight of an officer can produce either a warm sense of safety and contentment or a plummeting feeling of terror.

I've really felt the latter only once, at the 2000 Republican National Convention. I was twenty-one years old. My then-girlfriend-now-wife's father, Andy Shaw, a journalist, was covering the convention, and she and I decided to head to Philadelphia, both to see him and to take in the sights and sounds of thousands of Republicans assembling to nominate George W. Bush for president. After a train ride down from New York, we met Andy outside the convention center. Kate and I drew stares from convention delegates who were in country club attire, since we were dressed like the scruffy college students we were. People asked if we were protesters.

The three of us began to make our way through the multilayered security checkpoints. At the first one, as we put our bags through a metal detector, I suddenly remembered that I happened to have about thirty dollars worth of marijuana stuffed into my eyeglass case in a side pocket of my travel bag.

Luckily the bag went through the metal detector with no problems, and as I picked it back up, I smiled to myself in relief at my near miss. But then the security line continued, and we passed through another checkpoint, and another. We finally rounded a bend to find yet *another* group of Philadelphia cops, with another metal detector; worst of all, this group seemed to be rifling through every bag.

I felt a pulsing in my temples as I watched an officer open the main pocket of my bag and search. Then he opened the second pocket and finally the side pocket with my eyeglass case. He reached in and was about to put it back in when he stopped and gave it a shake, realizing there was something inside.

He opened it, and his head jerked back in surprise at what

he'd just found. He quickly turned his back to me and called over two other cops, one on each side. The three of them stood shoulder to shoulder, huddled, discussing.

My vision started to peel in at the corners, and I felt briefly possessed. I envisioned running; it seemed tantalizingly possible. Liberating. I could get away before they had any idea who I was or whose bag it was. Did I have anything identifying in there? I must've.

But then, my girlfriend and her father were standing right there, so flight probably wouldn't work. With tremendous effort, I overrode the impulse. "I think the cops just found weed in my bag," I whispered to Kate. And then in desperation, searching for someone to fix the situation, or at the very least to absolve me of this idiotic mistake, I walked over to my future father-in-law and blurted out, "Andy, I think the cops just found weed in my bag."

The cops continued to confer ominously.

Andy was confused. "What? Why'd you bring weed?"

And at that very moment, before I could answer (and really, what could I have said?), the police officer who'd found the drugs put my bag on a table and looked at me, as if to say *Go ahead and take it.*

I figured as soon as I reached out and acknowledged the bag was mine, they'd slap the cuffs on. But when I went to grab the bag . . . nothing happened. I picked it up.

Kate, her dad, and I walked into the convention center together. Her father said, amusedly, "You probably shouldn't do that tomorrow."

Out of morbid curiosity, I went into the first bathroom inside the arena, fished out my glasses case, and flipped it open. Sure enough, the weed was still there.

This story is one of my better ones. "The time I almost got caught with drugs at the Republican National Convention" is fun to tell because, ultimately, nothing bad came out of it. And with the advantage of hindsight, I can look back and know that even if I had been arrested, it would've been no more than an embarrassing hassle. I'm a straight white guy. I was a college student. I had access to lawyers and resources and, through all that, a very good chance of convincing someone that the world would keep spinning on its axis if I pleaded to a misdemeanor and got a little probation, and we all just pretended it hadn't happened.

Luckily for me, that harrowing encounter is the closest I've come to the criminal justice system. But over the past several years, I've spent a lot of time on the ground reporting both on criminal justice and on the growing social movement to change how it operates. And in hundreds of conversations with people in Baltimore, Charleston, Chicago, New York, Ferguson, Dallas, and elsewhere, I've had occasion to think about the enormous distance between their experience of the law and my own.

On a warm October day on the Westside of Baltimore, I stood interviewing Dayvon Love in the parking lot of a public school where he once coached debate. I was there to talk about policing and crime and the trauma of lives lived dodging both with no cover.

Earlier that year, in April, a young man named Freddie
Gray had died in police custody. His death triggered public mourning, calls for official resignations, protests, and
unrest. The city was now bracing for the trials of the officers
who had been indicted for causing Gray's death. (None of
them would be convicted. Midway through a succession of
trials, after a hung jury and a mistrial for one officer and
three acquittals, the prosecutor would throw in the towel
and drop the rest of the charges.)

Love was a good person to have that conversation with. He
speaks with an uncanny and particular cadence that comes
from a life steeped in competitive debate. Born poor on the
Westside, he discovered debate as a teenager through a program in his school and got hooked. "My initial motivation
was that I needed to get into college for free," he says when
I ask what led him to debate. "So I just thought, 'I am going
to get really good at this so I can go to college for free,' and
that's what happened. But along the way I was able to meet
people who helped me think about debate as a broader tool
for social justice."

Today Love coaches high school debate on the Westside
and works as a political activist. His 2008 debating team,
composed entirely of black students from one of Baltimore's
most impoverished neighborhoods, won the national cham-
pionship. Run-ins with police were simply part of life in his
neighborhood, Love told me, and no amount of bookish-
ness or respectability was a shield.

One night his life almost changed. "I was seventeen years

old, it was the day of a debate tournament. I'd won first place, and that night I was catching a bus to go to New York to see a friend." He had met the New York friend through Model UN just a few weeks earlier. On his way to the bus station in the wee hours of the morning, Love and his father were pulled over by police. "They say I match the description of someone who stole a woman's purse."

The police began to search the car. More cruisers pulled up with their lights flashing. They took Love out of the car and had him stand in the middle of the street. At one point, one shined his police light right into the teenager's face "And you heard them ask the woman, you know, 'Is this him'? And she says, 'I don't know.' And so luckily I had the presence of mind to think, 'We had just stopped at the ATM to get the money I needed for my ticket.' So I explained to them, I said I had just got the money that I needed to pay for my ticket." Love happened to have the receipt from the ATM; the time stamp corroborated his story. "And luckily they let me get away, but that easily could have went in an entirely different way."

By "entirely different way," Love meant being swept into the vortex of a penal system that captures more than half the black men his age in his neighborhood. By "entirely different way," he meant an adulthood marked by prison, probation, and dismal job prospects rather than debate coaching and activism. If he hadn't been so quick on his feet, if the woman hadn't been unsure the police had the right person, everything might have been different.

Fair to say that Dayvon and I, in our ways, both dodged a bullet, but the similarities ended there. I actually did something wrong: I was carrying an illegal drug. I wasn't quick enough on my feet to defuse the situation, and even if I had been arrested and booked, it all almost certainly would have worked out fine in the end. The stakes felt very high, but they were actually pretty low.

Dayvon, on the other hand, had done nothing wrong. Unlike me, he *was* quick enough on his feet to successfully defuse the situation. And while for me the stakes were in reality rather low, for him they weren't. Everything really could have changed in that moment for the worse. Out of those two brushes with the law, we both ended up with the same outcome: a clean record and a sigh of relief. But it took vastly different degrees of effort and ingenuity to get there.

THE UNITED STATES IS the most violent developed country in the world. It is also the most incarcerated. For more than four decades the second problem has grown, often under the guise of addressing the first. While the country's homicide rate has fallen sharply from its peak, it remains higher than that of any other developed democracy, sandwiched between Estonia and Chile in international rankings. America imprisons a higher percentage of its citizens than any other country, free or unfree, anywhere in the world, except the tiny archipelago of Seychelles. The total number of Americans under penal supervision, some have argued, even rivals the number of Russians in the gulag under Stalin. Nearly one out of every four prisoners in the world is an American, though the United States has just 5 percent of the world's population.

If you move in affluent, white, elite social circles, you probably know these statistics but never really see them in action. In the world's most punitive criminal system, the application of punishment is uneven in the extreme. Black men aged 20 to 34 without a high school degree have an institutionalization rate of about 37 percent. For white men without a high school degree, it's 12 percent, or nearly three times lower. In Sandtown-Winchester, which is 96.6 percent black and is the small slice of West Baltimore where Freddie Gray lived and died, there were, in February 2015, 458 people in prison. In Greater Roland Park/Poplar Hill, an affluent Baltimore neighborhood that is 77.5 percent white, there was a grand total of three.

Just as punishment is unequally distributed, so too is violence. Within the same city, the threat of violent death from homicide is radically unequal across different neighborhoods. Chicago has many affluent, predominantly white neighborhoods on the North Side where the murder rate is less 1 per 100,000. But on the city's poor, predominantly black South Side, several neighborhoods have a homicide rate that is 9,000 percent higher. On the whole, across the country, African Americans are victims of homicide at a rate of nearly 20 per 100,000. For whites, the rate is 2.5. Put another way: for white Americans, lethal violence is nearly as rare as it is in Finland; for black Americans, it's nearly as common as it is in Mexico. So to talk about the American experience of crime and punishment is to miss the point. Though Dayvon and I are both Americans, we live in different countries.

Different systems of justice are a centuries-old American tradition, indeed a foundational one. But the particular system we have now—the sprawling alternative state of jails, prisons, probation, penal supervision, warrants, "stop and frisk," "broken windows" policing, and the all-too-frequent shooting of the unarmed—dates back to the late 1960s.

Three things happened in the 1960s to shape the politics of how and upon whom we enforce law. The first was the success of the civil rights movement in beginning to dislodge decades of Jim Crow and crack open the vise of American racial hierarchy. This hard-fought success also produced intense, even violent white backlash, widespread fragility, and resentment at the social order being unmade.

The second was a once-in-a-century crime rate increase that would last several decades. The scope of this social upheaval is difficult to overstate. In 1965, the year of the Watts riots, there were 387,390 violent crimes in a nation with a population of about 194 million. By 1979, the number of violent crimes jumped more than 300 percent to 1,208,030, in a country whose population increased by only about 15 percent. The trend would continue until 1992, the year the country set an all-time violent crime record with 1,932,274 incidents. The great crime wave showed up in almost every geographical area in the country and across every category of crime, from rape to murder, assault to larceny. Nothing quite like it had ever happened before.

Any social indicator that rose as rapidly as crime did would rightly be seen as a national crisis. If the number of people who died in car crashes doubled in ten years or if inflation went up 750 percent in thirty-five years, our politics would demand some response. So the question in the late 1960s wasn't so much *if* something would be done but *what* would be done.

The third thing was that even as white backlash was gaining strength and crime was on the rise, street protests were exploding. In 1965 the unrest and police response in Watts left thirty-four dead. In 1967 twenty-three people were killed in Detroit following a police raid on a speakeasy. More uprisings followed in 1968 after the assassination of Martin Luther King, Jr., resulting in forty-three people killed in riots throughout the nation.

There are many theories as to why crime exploded during this period, and they vary significantly in their persuasiveness, but what mattered most *politically* was how easily politicians and then voters were able to make the connection between the unraveling of order and the violations of law. When people are allowed to take over the streets in protest, what's to stop them from robbing and stealing and killing?

In 1968 Richard Nixon ran for U.S. president making precisely this argument. When he appeared before the del-

egates of the Republican National Convention in Miami
to accept their nomination, he offered a grim vision. "As
we look at America, we see cities enveloped in smoke and
flame," he said. "We hear sirens in the night. . . . We see
Americans hating each other; fighting each other; killing
each other at home."

As Nixon spoke, the war in Vietnam was in its deadliest
phase, protests against it larger and more militant than
ever, Martin Luther King was dead, black power was ascen-
dant, and riots continued to rage from coast to coast. Nixon
assured the delegates and the voters watching at home that
"the wave of crime is not going to be the wave of the future
in the United States of America."

"Tonight," Nixon said, "it is time for some honest talk
about the problem of order in the United States." He spoke
amid an unfolding rights revolution in the nation's courts,
with the U.S. Supreme Court, under Chief Justice Earl Warren, strengthening the rights of criminal defendants as
never before, most famously in its 1966 *Miranda* decision.
Nixon argued that things had gotten out of whack. "Let us
always respect, as I do, our courts and those who serve on
them. But let us also recognize that some of our courts in
their decisions have gone too far in weakening the peace
forces as against the criminal forces in this country and we
must act to restore that balance."

Today liberals tend to think of Nixon's 1968 campaign
as fueled primarily by potent racial backlash. But Nixon
understood that the majority of Americans viewed them-

selves as fair and freedom-loving and would reject rhetoric that sounded too overtly authoritarian. He recognized that his best bet was to cultivate white resentment with coded appeals, wrapped in gracious displays of equanimity and high-minded rhetoric about equality. He even went out of his way to address his critics who accused him of using dog whistles. "To those who say law and order is the code word for racism," he said, "there and here is a reply: Our goal is justice for every American. If we are to have respect for law in America, we must have laws that deserve respect."

Nixon's genius in 1968 was to reach back to the Founders and somehow find in that revolutionary generation a call for order. "The American Revolution was and is dedicated to progress, but our founders recognized that the first requisite of progress is order," he said. "Now, there is no quarrel between progress and order—because neither can exist without the other." In fact, "the first civil right of every American is to be free from domestic violence, and that right must be guaranteed in this country."

This rhetoric and framing would become the template to justify forty years of escalating incarceration: *Order is necessary for liberty to flourish. If we do not have order, we can have no other rights.* It would dominate the politics of both parties over the next three decades, as crime continued to climb. Fear for one's own body against a violent predator, for the sanctity and safety of one's hearth against incursions by the depraved—these kinds of political issues operate far below the frontal cortex, deep beneath the dry talk of policy or tax rates. They are primal and primary. And in America, when the state cultivates such fear among relatively empowered white voters, it is enriching uranium for a political nuclear weapon.

It was Ferguson, Missouri, that made me understand the sheer seductive magnetism of this simple idea. On the Thursday in August 2014 after Michael Brown was shot and killed, I was sitting in a car trying to pull out of a parking lot onto the town's main thoroughfare and having no luck. The street was knotted with cars, lights blinking and horns honking. Young people sat on top of SUVs waving signs and blasting music. The scene wasn't a protest so much as an impromptu street festival, a victory parade. Just two nights earlier about a hundred protesters had been met by dozens of heavily armed police from the surrounding areas, aiming assault weapons from their tactical vehicles. The ensuing events—seen through the lens of a smartphone—had had the air of warfare, or, more perniciously, the brutality of a third world dictatorship. Images like the instantly iconic photo of a young black man in dreads, hands raised in surrender in the face of six cops in camouflage and gas masks pointing their rifles at him, had so embarrassed the political class of Missouri that Governor Jay Nixon had ordered a black state trooper named Captain Ron Johnson to take over. His response was to massively scale back police presence, leading to this triumphant festival atmosphere.

The scene before me was peaceful and, by and large, lawful: some weed here and there, but for the most part people were just partying. But if it was mostly lawful, it was not at all orderly. Traffic was snarled, horns and music were blaring, and people drank from open containers, as crowds threaded through the standstill traffic. Some deep, neurotic part of me took in the scene with unease, and I recalled the hostile questions Governor Nixon had faced from local reporters earlier that day at his press conference. While most of the national and international press corps had grilled Nixon on the garish spectacle of police officers equipped for war against a few dozen nonviolent protesters, the local press was attacking him from the other direction. Was the governor just going to abandon the streets to the thugs? Was he going to let Ferguson burn, as it had that first night after Brown's death? Wasn't he going to maintain *order*?

As a few of my producers from MSNBC and I managed to pull between two cars and make a left away from the madness, I felt a new understanding of the phrase "law and order." I'd always thought its political appeal lay in the law and all that that term meant: a nation of laws not of men; equal justice under law; the rule of law. But I realized in that moment that the phrase's power lay in the second term, in the promise of order, where people walk on the sidewalks, not in the street; traffic flows smoothly; and music is played softly and discreetly. In Ferguson that order was being boisterously, furiously, fuck-you'ed. And the beneficiaries of that order—from the local reporters to the homeowners in leafy seclusion just a few blocks away—looked on in horror. I could sense their anxiety almost telepathically.

Richard Nixon identified the problem America faced in 1968 as fundamentally a lack of order. And really who— black or white—can be against order? Who can stand against tranquility? Part of the genius of the rhetoric of law and order is that as a principle (rather than a practice), it can be sold as the ultimate call for equality: *We all deserve the law. We all deserve order. All lives matter.*

But even if the rhetoric of order is the most enduring legacy of Nixon's 1968 convention speech, that's not, to my mind, the speech's most important theme. Nixon under- stood that black demands for equality had to be acknowl- edged and given their rhetorical due. He promised "a new policy for peace and progress and justice at home," and pledged that his new attorney general would "be an active belligerent against the loan sharks and the numbers rack- eteers that rob the urban poor in our cities." "And let us build bridges, my friends," he offered, "build bridges to human dignity across that gulf that separates black America from white America. Black Americans, no more than white Americans, they do not want more government programs which perpetuate dependency. *They don't want to be a colony in a nation.*"

A colony in a nation.

Nixon meant to conjure an image of a people reduced to mere recipients of state handouts rather than active citizens shaping their own lives. And in using the image of a colony, he was, in his own odd way, channeling the zeitgeist. As anti- colonial movements erupted in the 1960s, colonized people across the globe recognized a unity of purpose between their own struggles for self-determination and the struggle of black Americans. Black activists, in turn, recognized their own plight in the images of colonial subjects fighting an oppressive white government. America's own colonial history was quite different from that of, say, Rhodesia, but on the ground the structures of oppression looked remarkably similar.

In fact, when Nixon invoked "a colony in a nation" black activists and academics were in the midst of extended debate about the concept of internal colonialism and whether the state of black people in America was akin to a colonized people. A year earlier Stokely Carmichael and Charles V. Hamilton published *Black Power*, which argued explicitly that America's ghettos were colonized and occupied and that black nationalism was the only route to true liberation. The concept had long roots: in 1935, W. E. B. DuBois had written of black people as a "nation within a nation." Over the years, critics of the concept have noted the weaknesses of the framework in accounting for the distinct economic situation of African Americans and the changes in their representation and situation over time.

But whatever the academic debate on the topic, Nixon was correct that black Americans "don't want to be a colony in a nation." And yet he helped bring about that very thing. Over the half-century since he delivered those words, we have built a colony in a nation, not in the classic Marxist sense but in the deep sense we can appreciate as a former colony ourselves: A territory that isn't actually free. A place

controlled from outside rather than within. A place where
the mechanisms of representation don't work enough to
give citizens a sense of ownership over their own government. A place where the law is a tool of control rather than
a foundation for prosperity. A political regime like the one
our Founders inherited and rejected. An order they spilled
their blood to defeat.

THIS BOOK MAKES A simple argument: that American criminal justice isn't one system with massive racial disparities
but two distinct regimes. One (the Nation) is the kind of
policing regime you expect in a democracy; the other (the
Colony) is the kind you expect in an occupied land. Policing
is a uniquely important and uniquely dangerous function
of the state.* Dictatorships and totalitarian regimes use the
police in horrifying ways; we call them "police states" for a
reason. But the terrifying truth is that we as a people have
created the Colony through democratic means. We have
voted to subdue our fellow citizens; we have rushed to the
polls to elect people promising to bar others from enjoy-
ing the fruits of liberty. A majority of Americans have put a
minority under lock and key.

* As sociologist Max Weber argued in *Politics as a Vocation* (1919),
the state is the one institution that has a monopoly on the legitimate
use of violence.

In her masterful 2010 chronicle of American mass incarceration, *The New Jim Crow*, Michelle Alexander argues convincingly that our current era represents not a shift from previous eras of white supremacy and black oppression but continuity with them. After the 1960s, she contends, when Jim Crow was dismantled as a legal entity, it was reconceived and reborn through mass incarceration. "Rather than rely on race," she writes, "we use our criminal justice system to label people of color 'criminals' and then engage in all the practices we supposedly left behind. . . . As a criminal, you have scarcely more rights, and arguably less respect, than a black man living in Alabama at the height of Jim Crow. We have not ended racial caste in America; we have merely redesigned it."

As I covered the unrest in Ferguson, Alexander's analysis seemed undeniable. Clearly the police had taken on the role of enforcing an unannounced but very real form of segregation in the St. Louis suburb. Here was a town that was born of white flight and segregation, nestled in a group of similar hamlets that were notoriously "sundown towns," where southern police made sure black people didn't tarry or stay the night. And despite the fact that Ferguson's residents were mostly black, the town's entire power structure was white, from the mayor, to the city manager, to all but one school board member as well as all but one city council member, and to the police chief and the police force itself, which had three black cops out of fifty-three.

Then just eight months later I was on the streets of Baltimore after yet another young black man died at the hands of police, and the stories and complaints I heard from the residents there sounded uncannily like those I'd heard in Ferguson. But if Ferguson's unrest was clearly the result of a total lack of black political power, that didn't seem to be the case, at least not at first look, in Baltimore: the city had black city council members, a black mayor, a very powerful black member of Congress, a black state's attorney, and a police force that was integrated.

If Ferguson looked like Jim Crow, Baltimore was something else. The old Jim Crow comprised twin systems of oppression: segregation across public and private spheres that kept black people away from social and economic equality, and systematic political disenfranchisement that made sure black citizens weren't represented democratically. These twin systems required two separate pieces of landmark legislation to destroy, the 1964 Civil Rights Act and the 1965 Voting Rights Act.

Through ceaseless struggle and federal oversight, the civil rights movement ended de jure segregation and created the legal conditions for black elected political power—state representatives, black mayors, city council members, black police chiefs, even a few black senators and a black president. But this power has turned out to be strikingly confined and circumscribed, incorporated into the maintenance of order through something that looks—in many places—more like the centuries-old model of colonial administration.

From India to Vietnam to the Caribbean, colonial systems have always integrated the colonized into government power, while still keeping the colonial subjects in their place.

Half the cops accused of killing Freddie Gray were black; half were white. The Baltimore police chief is black, as is the mayor. And Freddie Gray, the figure upon whom this authority was wielded?

Well, to those in the neighborhood, there was never any question what race he would be.

In the era of the First Black President, black political power has never been more fully realized, and yet for so many black people blackness feels just as dangerous as ever. Black people can live and even prosper in the Nation, but they can never be truly citizens. The threat of the Colony's nightstick always lingers, even for, say, a famous and distinguished Harvard professor of African American studies who suddenly found himself in handcuffs on his own stately porch just because someone thought he was a burglar.

Race defines the boundaries of the Colony and the Nation, but race itself is a porous and shifting concept. Whiteness is nonexistent, yet it confers enormous benefits. Blackness is a conjured fiction, yet it is so real it can kill. In their brilliant 2012 collection of essays, *Racecraft: The Soul of Inequality in American Life,* Karen and Barbara Fields trace the semantic trick of racial vocabulary, which *invents* categories for the purpose of oppression while appearing to *describe* things that already exist out in the world. Over time these categories shift, both as reflections of those in power and as expressions of solidarity and resistance in the face of white supremacy.

Because our racial categories are always shifting, morphing, disappearing, and reappearing, so too are the borders between the Colony and the Nation. In many places, the two territories alternate block by block, in a patchwork of unmarked boundaries and detours that are known only by those who live within them. It's like the fictional cities of Besźel and Ul Qoma in China Miéville's gorgeous speculative fantasy detective novel *The City & the City*. Though the cities occupy the same patch of land, each city's residents discipline themselves to unsee the landscape of their neighbor's city.

The two-block stretch where Michael Brown lived and died in Ferguson, the low-rise apartments home to Section 8 tenants that the mayor told me had been a "problem," is part of the Colony. The farmers' market a half-mile away, where the mayor was when Brown was shot, is part of the Nation. The west side of Cleveland where twelve-year-old Tamir Rice was shot and killed while playing in a park is part of the Colony. The Westside of Baltimore, where Dayvon Love grew up and Freddie Gray died, is part of the Colony. The South Side of Chicago, where Laquan McDonald was shot and killed, is too.

This is the legacy of a post-civil-rights social order that gave up on desegregation as a guiding mission and accepted a country of de facto segregation between "nice neighborhoods" and "rough neighborhoods," "good schools" and "bad schools," "inner cities" and "bedroom communities."

None of this came about by accident. It was the result of accumulation of policy, from federal housing guidelines and realtor practices to the decisions of tens of thousands of school boards and town councils and homeowners' associations essentially drawing boundaries: the Nation on one side, the Colony on the other.

In the Colony, violence looms, and failure to comply can be fatal. Sandra Bland, a twenty-eight-year-old black woman who died in a Texas prison cell in July 2015, was pulled over because she didn't signal a lane change. Walter Scott, the fifty-year-old black man shot in the back three months earlier as he fled a North Charleston police officer, was pulled over because one of the three brake lights on his newly purchased car was out. Freddie Gray, the twenty-five-year-old resident of one of Baltimore's poorest neighborhoods whose spinal cord was snapped in a police van, simply made eye contact with a police officer and started to move swiftly in the other direction.

If you live in the Nation, the criminal justice system functions like your laptop's operating system, quietly humming in the background, doing what it needs to do to allow you to be your most efficient, functional self. In the Colony, the system functions like a computer virus: it intrudes constantly, it interrupts your life at the most inconvenient times, and it does this as a matter of course. The disruption itself is normal.

In the Nation, there is law; in the Colony, there is only

a concern with order. In the Nation, you have rights; in the Colony, you have commands. In the Nation, you are innocent until proven guilty; in the Colony, you are born guilty. Police officers tasked with keeping these two realms separate intuitively grasp of the contours of this divide: as one Baltimore police sergeant instructed his officers, "Do not treat criminals like citizens."

In the Nation, you can stroll down the middle of a quiet, carless street with no hassle, as I did with James Knowles, the white Republican mayor of Ferguson. We chatted on a leafy block in a predominantly white neighborhood filled with stately Victorian homes and wraparound porches. There were no cops around. We were technically breaking the law—you can't walk in the middle of the street—but no one was going to enforce that law, because really what's the point. Who were we hurting?

In the Colony, just half a mile away, the disorderly act of strolling down the middle of the street could be the first link in the chain of events that ends your life at the hands of the state.

The Colony is overwhelmingly black and brown, but in the wake of financial catastrophe, deindustrialization, and sustained wage stagnation, the tendencies and systems of control developed in the Colony have been deployed over wider and wider swaths of working-class white America. If you released every African American and Latino prisoner in America's prisons, the United States would still be one of the most incarcerated societies on earth. And the makeup of those white prisoners is dramatically skewed toward the poor and uneducated. As of 2008, nearly 15 percent of white high school dropouts aged 20 to 34 were in prison. For white college grads, the rate was under 1 percent.

Maintaining the division between the Colony and the Nation is treacherous precisely because the constant threat that the tools honed in the Colony will be wielded in the Nation; that tyranny and violence tolerated at the periphery will ultimately infiltrate the core. American police shoot an alarmingly high and disproportionate number of black people. But they also shoot a shockingly large number of white people.

Even the most sympathetic residents of the Nation, I think, find it easy to think this is all someone else's problem. Yes, of course, America is overincarcerated, of course the police killing unarmed black men is awful, and yes, of course I'd like to see all that change. But it's fundamentally someone else's issue.

It's not.

Here's why.

The images in the video are blurry and dark—a scene that has the jagged uneasiness of something you shouldn't be seeing. Voices on the edge of panic and brimming with rage discuss the uniformed men who are marching into view. In the smartphone's shaky frame, you can start to make out the invaders in silhouette against a vehicle's flashing lights. Lots of shouts now from the onlookers who are seeing the same image coming into view. The marching men are dressed in black, and as they come closer, you can see they are wearing armor. Bulges at the knees. Shields in hand. They stroll casually. The street is empty, but the bystanders, standing in their yard sipping from plastic cups, begin chanting at them: "*You* go home! *You* go home! *You* go home!"

One of the bystanders narrates the unfolding scene into the phone. "They are marching toward us. You can see 'em coming, and they are marching toward us." At this point the viewer sees many more men in armor than had first appeared. Maybe three dozen in a walking wedge formation are making their way up the street. They are not in a hurry. Those congregated in the yard chant "Hands up! Don't shoot!" The camera pans to the yard as four young men, one holding a drink, reach up in to the air, chanting "Hands up!" in unison.

A few nights earlier in this neighborhood a police officer named Darren Wilson had shot and killed a young man named Michael Brown. Brown was unarmed. The friend who was with him, and several other eyewitnesses, said he had had his hands up* when he was shot. In the following days, protests erupted, a gas station was burned, police came out in shockingly heavy force, and those who took to the streets united around the chant "Hands up! Don't shoot!"

The young men in the yard are now hit by the high beams of a police vehicle. Through the loudspeaker, it sounds as if the cops tell them to "go home," and they respond "We in our yard!" pointing to the ground beneath their feet for emphasis. The men in the yard raise their hands defiantly, as the loudspeaker instructs them "Please return inside," with

---

* In a later Department of Justice investigation, other eyewitnesses said Brown did *not* have his hands up and in fact was moving toward Officer Wilson and "appeared to pose a physical threat" to him. Ultimately the Department of Justice would conclude that the claims of Brown having his hands up were not consistent with the "physical and forensic evidence."

the same oddly laconic pacing of the armed men marching toward them. The residents stand defiantly with hands up, as someone off camera angrily calls the police's bluff: "Go head, shoot that motherfucker. Shoot that motherfucker!"

Another says, "C'mon. You want it. Come get it. You want it. Come get it."

His friend yells, "This my property!" and points again down at the ground as the camera pans to reveal the police have now come within about twenty feet.

And then: a brief flare, and the screen goes dark.

Bedlam. Screams. The person holding the camera appears to hit the ground.

The camera returns upright and shows clouds of gas where the cops had been, with the lights glowing eerily behind them. The man who said he owns the house appears apoplectic. The police just shot a gas canister into his yard! He hops around the frame in rage, pointing down again at the ground "This my shit! This my shit! No, fuck that shit!"

A friend comes to escort him away from confronting the phalanx of cops as he continues to yell, "This my shit!"

Then: "You got all this recorded? This my backyard!"

"This what they do to us!"

"This my backyard!"

"This is our home. This is our residence."

The man who appears to be the homeowner yells back to the cops, "Now go the fuck home!"

And then his friend turns to the camera and asks "Why do you think people say 'Fuck the police'?"

He points back at the smoke still wafting in the background.

"This shit."

WHEN A COP TELLS you to do something, do it. You hear this folk wisdom a lot, and it basically comes in two varieties. The first version is the central lesson of the Talk that so many African American parents give their children about how to survive a police encounter. Practical advice: Keep your hands on the wheel. Don't make sudden movements. Say "Yes, officer. No, officer." Et cetera.

The other version of this folk wisdom isn't merely practical advice but reflects a deeper belief about the sanctity of police authority. It's what lies behind the question you so often hear: *Why didn't she just do what the cop said?* That inquiry comes unbidden every single time some incident of police violence is captured on video. Even when the citizen in question is, say, a sixteen-year-old foster child sitting at her desk in her classroom in Columbia, South Carolina, refusing to leave, only to be body slammed and dragged across the room. *Why didn't she just comply?* and *None of this would have happened if she'd just listened.*

Section 29-16(1) of the municipal code of the city of Ferguson, Missouri, codifies this principle. It is a crime to "[f]ail to comply with the lawful order or request of a police officer in the discharge of the officer's official duties." As the Department of Justice would later show, the police much abuse this statute. Ferguson cops routinely issue orders that have no legal basis and then arrest citizens who refuse those orders for "failure to comply." It's a neat little circular bit of authoritarian reasoning.

In the video, the police order the onlookers to go back inside their homes. When the men in the yard refuse to comply, the police shoot tear gas at them. But can the police do that? Don't you have a right to stand in your own front yard? Thirteen years before the Declaration of Independence, British member of Parliament William Pitt defended the rights of Englishmen to privacy in their own home. He declared: "The poorest man may in his cottage bid defiance to all the forces of the Crown. It may be frail; its roof may shake; the wind may blow through it; the storm may enter; the rain may enter; but the King of England cannot enter—all his forces dare not cross the threshold of the ruined tenement!"

In modern parlance: *This is our home. This is our residence.*

Like the vast majority of national reporters who descended on Ferguson in August 2014, I had no idea of the place's existence until the night of August 9, when reports started circulating on Twitter that a young unarmed black man had been shot and killed there.

A few days into the unrest that followed, an Iraq war vet tweeted a photo of himself next to one of a cop on the streets of Ferguson, noting, "The gentleman on the left has more personal body armor and weaponry than I did while invading Iraq." Not just that: the cops in Ferguson were clad in head-to-toe camouflage, as if the olive and sandy brown color scheme would help them blend into the McDonald's parking lot they were patrolling.

The events on the streets of Ferguson in the days after Brown's death didn't outrage black people alone—it spooked people of all races. People who'd never had occasion to personally distrust the police wondered what the hell weapons of war were doing on the streets of this small St. Louis suburb. Politicians from both parties raised their voices to express concern, and to urge restraint, as the nightly news carried images of the kinds of disorder—tear gas, riot gear, clashes with police—that we normally associate with countries where the government sends in armed troops to put down dissidents, or where the possibility of all-out war does not seem remote.

Of course none of this would have happened, some argued, if protesters had done what they were told. If everyone had listened to the police, everything could have continued as it always had.

Societies operate through formal procedures of law and force but also through norms of compliance. Without those norms, nothing would function. Suppose you want to make a left-hand turn, but a traffic cop says you can't. You don't ask her to cite the law—you just don't make the turn. You assume there's a good reason for her to be blocking that street. Maybe there's been an accident. Maybe there's a fire. Or maybe there will be less traffic, and things will be more orderly, if she keeps you and everyone else from making a left at rush hour. Fine. Fair enough. Do what the cop says.

But as a principle of self-governance, particularly of *American* self-governance, "do what the cops say" is a pretty strange unofficial motto. This great land of ours, this exceptional beacon of liberty, was founded by men who, to borrow a phrase, refused to comply. Who not only resisted lawful orders but rebelled against the government that issued them. Colonists chased the king's officers through the streets, caught them, beat them, tarred and feathered them, and wheeled them through town for all to mock and shame. As distant as it may seem now, that's our national heritage when it comes to "lawful orders."

SEVERAL MORNINGS AFTER MICHAEL BROWN was shot and killed, and a group of angry youths burned down the local Quick Trip gas station, I ran into a few gentlemen assembled in that same burned-out parking lot, arguing and talking about politics as they cleaned up the site. One man in his fifties, with a wiry intensity, looked into the camera I had with me and said, "We want the world to know that we are a dignified, intelligent people, and we deserve every liberty that the United States Constitution affords any citizen."

But what was the Constitution doing, really, in Ferguson? It seemed an absurdly remote abstraction, as practical a piece of protection as reciting a poem into the barrel of a gun. And yet in a grand irony the document itself, and the nation it binds together, was born of almost the exact same set of grievances as those of the protesters getting tear-gassed in the streets of Ferguson.

We are taught in grade school that the motto of the America Revolution was "No taxation without representation." The tyrannical King George III insisted on taxing the colonies against their will, employing ever more draconian measures to do so, until the colonists could take it no longer.

The idea that unjust taxation triggered the American uprising stays with us (or at least it stayed with me). But dig a little deeper into the history, and it turns out the spark of the revolution was not so much taxation as the *enforcement* of a particular tax regime—in other words, policing.

Today the word *taxes* conjures up images of our modern administrative state, with automatic payroll deductions, marginal brackets, and sales tax, a system in which the collection of taxes is a bureaucratic affair. But that image fails to capture what taxation meant in the colonies at the time of the revolution. Under the British colonial system (and indeed for the first century of the United States), the lion's share of taxes was assessed as tariffs: duties imposed on those wishing to import or export goods. These tariffs were central to the entire colonial system erected by England and other empires during the era of mercantilist trade wars that dominated the seventeenth to nineteenth centuries.

Under British law (codified in the Navigation Acts), merchants and consumers in the colonies had to import nearly all of their products from British companies and pay very steep tariffs to do it. While Adam Smith would show, in *The Wealth of Nations* (published the same year as the Declaration of Independence), how self-defeating this system of trade ultimately was, to the mercantilist empires at the time the logic was impeccable: colonies meant cheap commodity imports for the home country, a lucrative market for manufactured exports, and significant revenues through tariffs on all those exchanges. (The British would later employ this same logic to outlaw Indians on the subcontinent from making their own salt, or weaving their own garments, so they'd have to purchase both from their colonial ruler.)

So if you lived in the colonies and wanted to buy something that wasn't produced or grown there—whether tea to drink or the molasses your distillery needed to produce rum—you had to import it through the Crown and pay a steep tariff. And that's when you could actually get the thing you wanted. Often you couldn't, since many popular products weren't produced anywhere in the British Empire. Madeira wine was made in rival Portugal and became quite popular in the colonies, but it had to be smuggled in. (A shipment of Madeira would be at the heart of the 1768 *Liberty* Affair, an early skirmish over smuggling enforcement that would pave the way to the revolution. George Washington was a famous devotee of the beverage.)

In the American colonies, local shipping magnates provided illicit goods like Madeira. Despite their businesses' illegitimacy before British law, they were men of great wealth, prestige, and power. John Hancock, the man whose iconic signature dominates the founding documents, was one of the most infamous smugglers of his day. He was a criminal, basically—and he and his fellow smugglers kept the colonies running. Without the goods they smuggled, there would have been little local economy to speak of. Because the black market was so widespread, agents of the Crown tended to view the colonies as a den of iniquity, a seedy place overwhelmingly populated by hustlers, hucksters, and shady characters. One British officer referred to the residents of Newport, Rhode Island, one of the main smuggling hubs at the time and now a famous bastion of privilege, as "a set of lawless piratical people . . . whose sole business is that of smuggling and defrauding the King of his duties."

Much of that smuggling and defrauding centered on molasses, the raw ingredient needed for rum. Nearly all the molasses that American rum distilleries used to make their product came from Caribbean islands controlled by rival empires like the Dutch and the French. The demand for rum was bottomless, because rum was more than a drink. It was a kind of currency itself, a key commodity of exchange. Caribbean planters sent molasses north, the American colonies distilled the molasses into rum, and the rum was then sent across the Atlantic to the Gold Coast of Africa, where slavers used it to purchase slaves to bring back to the Caribbean.

Smuggling in the colonies was not so different from drug dealing in economically depressed neighborhoods and regions today. During the pre-Revolutionary era, smugglers created economic activity that caused huge knock-off effects: a cascade of subsidiary industries and cash flow that kept a whole lot of people in the colonies (not to mention lots of business back in merry old England) in the money. The same goes for dealers in, say, Westside Baltimore or the South Side of Chicago or the South Bronx, or northern Maine or eastern Kentucky or South Central Los Angeles. Sure, the drug trade is illegal, reckless, and destructive, but it encourages commerce in places where the legitimate economy produces few jobs. While dealers and "the street" are viewed skeptically, often angrily, they also command status. Dealers, like smugglers, become institutions—the way, say, New Englanders viewed John Hancock in the years leading to the revolution.

Such extensive criminal conspiracies depend and depended on codes of silence and the confidence that snitches will be punished. In 1759, when one informer in New York threatened to expose an illegal smuggling ring, a local official sympathetic to the smugglers arrested him on trumped-up charges, and an angry mob beat him to a pulp. Smuggling was so embedded in colonial society, British officers complained they couldn't find anyone to enforce the law who wasn't somehow connected to it. When they did manage to prosecute cases, they found that colonial juries engaged in their own version of nullification. Between 1680 and 1682 New England's head of customs brought thirty-two seizure cases to trial. He lost thirty.

The laws were unenforceable because the market demand was nearly limitless, and the colonies were an ocean away. And for much of the eighteenth century, the British Empire's attitude toward our Founders' rampant smuggling was one of benign neglect. The law was enforced in the same way drug laws are very loosely "enforced" on elite college campuses. Authorities know it's happening, but they don't go out of their way to bust people for it. Between 1710 and 1760, as the population of the colonies quintupled to over 1.5 million, the total number of customs agents rose from thirty-seven to fifty.

But then, as is so often the case, a war changed everything. Between 1754 and 1763 Britain fought a bloody and expensive campaign against the French and allied indigenous tribes in North America. As the so-called Seven Years' War dragged on, colonial officials watched in horror as smugglers openly flouted wartime laws that prohibited trading with the French enemy. When Britain signed the Treaty of Paris, ending the conflict, it gained much of Canada and Florida—but it had incurred a staggering amount of debt. The inexperienced young king, George III, turned to tariff enforcement in the colonies as a relatively painless way of replenishing the royal coffers. Or so he thought.

Because taxes were ultimately enforced through police actions, the British crackdown essentially inaugurated America's first tough-on-crime era. It was a classic crackdown: more customs officials were granted more expansive powers, while courts were streamlined to produce swift punishment and avoid the maddening jury nullification that had made it so hard to punish smugglers in previous decades. After 1763 customs officials no longer looked the other way in exchange for small bribes. Instead, they began operating in ways that looked a lot like what we now call "stop and frisk."

British customs officials took to trawling the coast, stopping merchant ships to search and harass them. Authorities had no specific cause for these searches other than their confidence that they'd find illicit goods. This was the same approach and justification that the NYPD infamously used to search for drugs and guns in the pockets of hundreds of thousands of young men, disproportionately black and brown, on the streets of New York in the 2000s. In a landmark legal ruling, a federal district judge found that "stop and frisk" amounted to wholesale, systematic violation of the Fourth Amendment protections against unwarranted search and seizure. "While it is true that any one stop is a limited intrusion in duration and deprivation of liberty, each stop is also a demeaning and humiliating experience," Judge Shira Scheindlin wrote in her opinion. "No one should live in fear of being stopped whenever he leaves his home to go about the activities of daily life."

The British legal tradition has no Fourth Amendment, but common law had developed some privacy protections. In the 1604 Semayne's Case, a British court ruled that the inhabitant of a house could rightfully bar the entry of a king's officer if the officer had not gone through the proper process. This case articulated the now-famous Castle Doctrine, with British jurist Sir Edward Coke declaiming, "The house of every one is to him as his castle and fortress, as well for his defense against injury and violence as for his repose."

But the American colonists were subject to British invasions of their carriages, ships, and homes without the safeguards enjoyed by their English cousins. Widely used "writs of assistance" allowed British officials to invade their homes willy-nilly, as part of a broader scheme to squeeze American pocketbooks. After the Seven Years' War, the hated writs of assistance empowered British customs officials to stop and search ships coming into New England ports.

You can imagine how insulting and humiliating the colonists found this arrangement. As subjects of the Crown, they felt entitled to the legal rights enjoyed by their brethren across the ocean, yet the king had functionally relegated them to second-class status. British subjects in Britain experienced one set of rights; British subjects in the colonies experienced a lesser set.

Late in his life John Adams reflected that the writs had bestowed upon any government official, no matter how lowly in the colonial order, the authority to rifle through the property of any colonist. Writs of assistance, he wrote,

> enable[d] the custom house officers . . . to command
> all sheriffs and constables to attend and aid them in
> breaking open houses, stores, shops, cellars, ships,
> bales, trunks, chests, casks, packages of all sorts, to

> search for goods, wares and merchandizes, which
> had been imported against the prohibitions.

The use of the writs was oppressive and disruptive. Every policing regime must choose just how tightly to enforce a given law, either explicitly or as the logical conclusion of other decisions. When citizens come to expect and understand a certain level of enforcement, they tailor their behavior accordingly. I have a keen sense that if I park in any of the various illegal spaces in my neighborhood, I'll probably get a ticket, and when I do, I understand it as the cost of the illegal action that I knowingly took. But if you're looking to make a community furious, then arbitrarily fiddle with enforcement norms, and see what happens.

As an example, imagine if suddenly the Cambridge, Massachusetts, authorities were to import the law enforcement approach used in central Harlem to police Harvard University. A massive police presence would be visible on every quad and in front of every dorm. Cops would stop and frisk students on their way to class; they would search the swank homes of parents of students caught with drugs; and they would monitor social media accounts to bust drug deals. The student body and their very powerful parents would revolt.

In the American colonies, the backlash was intense and only grew more so as British authorities—finding their efforts sabotaged and evaded—responded with ever more force.

At first the smugglers and their allies in the revolutionary hotbeds of New England port towns like Newport and

Boston mounted legal challenges. James Otis, Jr., a Harvard-
trained Boston lawyer and charismatic orator, rose to prom-
inence as the chosen advocate of the smuggler class. He
had been a lawyer for the colonial administration, initially
called upon to defend the writs of assistance, but rather
than do so, he resigned his post. In 1761, representing merchants pro bono, Otis appeared before the Superior Court
of Massachusetts to argue against the British use of writs of
assistance, calling them the "worst instrument of arbitrary
power, the most destructive of English liberty and the fundamental principles of law, that ever was found in an English law-book," and "a power that places the liberty of every
man in the hands of every petty officer."

His argument would stretch to five hours. John Adams,
who was among those who'd packed into the courthouse to
hear Otis, would later say:

> Every man of an immense crowded audience
> appeared to go away as I did, ready to take arms
> against writs of assistance. Then and there was the
> first scene of the first act of opposition to the arbi-
> trary rule of Great Britain. *Then and there the child
> Independence was born.*

Opposition to the crackdown wasn't limited to the
courts: petitions and pamphlets tumbled forth with ever-
mounting indignation and fury. Mob violence was a central
feature of the burgeoning revolutionary movement. Cus-

toms officials found themselves surrounded, jeered at, and harassed as they attempted to execute their official duties. Often mobs would simply steal back the confiscated contraband. Not surprisingly, the British did not take kindly to this behavior. They responded by doing everything short of declaring formal war on smugglers and on everyone who supported them.

The problem that King George III faced would bedevil authorities for centuries, from the revenuers of Prohibition to the modern Drug Enforcement Administration: when the state declares some popular good illicit, a good that enjoys widespread normalized usage, the state must pursue ever more draconian means to snuff it out.

As customs officials were granted more and more power to extinguish illicit trade, inevitably they began to abuse it. Often they actually made their money as a percentage of the value of the goods they confiscated, putting them in the same position as pirates, but with the entire force of the British Crown behind them. (It's not so different from today's police departments funding their budgets through civil forfeiture.) Abuse and corruption were widespread, and as enforcement ratcheted up, so did colonial hatred of the men doing the enforcing.

When extra customs officials proved insufficient to the task, the British authorities called in the navy. Now military vessels and sailors boarded and searched ships suspected of smuggling. The spectacle of this militarized policing enraged the colonists. Ben Franklin, with biting sarcasm,

attacked the folly of turning the tools of war-making on
civilians:

> Convert the brave, honest officers of your navy into
> pimping tide-waiters and colony officers of the cus-
> toms. Let those who in the time of war fought gal-
> lantly in defense of their countrymen, in peace be
> taught to prey upon it. Let them . . . scour with armed
> boats every bay, harbor, river, creek, cove, or nook
> throughout your colonies; stop and detain every
> coaster, every wood-boat, every fisherman. . . . Thus
> shall the trade of your colonists suffer more from
> their friends in time of peace, than it did from their
> enemies in war. . . . O, this will work admirably!

Animus built toward the most famous incident of the
pre-Revolutionary period, the Boston Tea Party. Like the
bromides about taxation and representation, the Boston
Tea Party doesn't actually make sense today without understanding the context of enforcement. The cargo dumped
from aboard several ships of the British East India Company
was legal tea. Contrary to what you may have learned, this
tea was relatively cheap for consumers to purchase, even
after including the price of the import tariff. The Crown
had granted the East India Company sole monopoly of the
import of this tea, making it the single legal competitor to the
vast armada of smugglers of illegal Dutch tea that flooded
the colonies. And in fact, what so enraged the revolution-

ary mob that defiled this shipment was that the Crown had recently *lowered* the import tariff on this legal tea, making it more economically competitive with smuggled tea. In other words, the Tea Party was triggered not by taxes being raised but rather by a tax *cut*. Our common understanding of the tea party as a revolt against taxes renders this basic truth invisible, but the event only makes sense in the broader context of an enforcement regime whose abuses and excesses had destroyed the government's legitimacy.

Escalating conflict between smugglers and the officers who policed smuggling was one of the chief drivers—perhaps *the* chief driver—toward the outbreak of violent insurgency that led to the country's founding. It was the point of the spear, where the inherent contradictions of colonial rule were made most acutely, painfully, and sometimes violently manifest. When the colonial insurrectionists railed against the king, it was his customs officers who embodied his tyranny. And sure enough, in the Declaration of Independence, in the list of petty indignities and offensive tyrannies of the Crown, we find an excoriation of the king for the fact the he has "sent hither swarms of officers to harass our people and eat out their substance."

SO WHAT DOES ALL of this have to do with Ferguson, Missouri? When you zoom out past the precipitating incident of Michael Brown's death and look at the Ferguson police as a whole, you find an enforcement regime strikingly similar to the British Crown's. The fundamental offense of British customs policing was that its driving rationale was revenue. Like the customs officers who interdicted smugglers to bring in tariffs, the police in Ferguson were ordered to write tickets to bring in money. That kind of law enforcement had nothing to do with public safety or welfare, and the public knew it. As the Department of Justice (DOJ) wrote in its report on the patterns and practices of the department:

> Ferguson's law enforcement practices are shaped by the City's focus on revenue rather than by public safety needs. This emphasis on revenue has compromised the institutional character of Ferguson's police department, contributing to a pattern of unconstitutional policing, and has also shaped its municipal court, leading to procedures that raise due process concerns and inflict unnecessary harm on members of the Ferguson community.

Like the regime in the American colonies, the enforcement regime in Ferguson had a lot to do with the lack of democratic accountability.

Here's a snapshot of Ferguson's history. It was built as a railroad town, but in the 1960s, as desegregation came to St. Louis schools, whites fled north from the city proper for the inner ring suburbs of St Louis County. Ferguson is just one of a number of surrounding municipalities that took in the influx of working-class whites. For a generation, the towns in St. Louis County were, in the words of one local, "white blue-collar Democrats. Military families. Union families."

And then in the inexorable migratory logic of white fear, when black people started to move into those same inner ring suburbs, whites who had been living there moved out farther into the sprawling exurbs. In 1990 Ferguson was 73 percent white and 25 percent black. A decade later African Americans were a slim majority, and by the time Michael Brown was shot and killed, African Americans comprised about two-thirds of the town's 21,000 residents. The white people who stayed had a certain pride in their own enlightenment and open-mindedness. "It's ironic this happened in Ferguson, because Ferguson had the reputation of being one of the most progressive [towns] in north St. Louis County," native Umar Lee told me. "Where you do have a strong contingent of white people . . . that are kind of committed to diversity, and you know, we've got the Ferguson farmers' market right down the street."

But if they are relatively enlightened, the white citizens of Ferguson are also disproportionately empowered: despite the fact they are a minority of the municipality, they dominate its political leadership.

In Ferguson, just about every single black person I spoke to had at least one story (often many) about humiliating traffic stops by Ferguson police officers that had nothing to do with public safety. And the statistics bear them out. In 2009, in a city of just 22,000, there were 24,000 traffic cases in the Ferguson municipal court, and by October 31, 2014, that figure had grown to 53,000. Nearly all levels of Ferguson's municipal government had pushed for the increase. In March 2010 the city's finance director warned the police chief, Tom Jackson, that "unless ticket writing ramps up significantly before the end of the year, it will be hard to significantly raise collections next year. What are your thoughts? Given that we are looking at a substantial sales tax shortfall, it's not an insignificant issue." By 2014, the year of Michael Brown's death, tickets and citations were still increasing as rapidly as they ever had. The DOJ found evidence that black residents of Ferguson received speeding tickets "at disproportionately high rates overall" and that the Ferguson police department's "enforcement practices on African Americans is 48% larger when citations are issued not on the basis of radar or laser, but by some other method, such as the officer's own visual assessment."

The model of cops as armed tax collectors didn't stop with simple traffic stops for speeding: the entire municipal court system was designed to function like a payday lending operation. Relatively small infractions quickly turned into massive debts. Many traffic citations required the ticketed person to make court appearances, but the local court would hold sessions only three to four times a month for just a few hours. Because of the limited hours, the court couldn't process everyone who came for their court date. Those left outside were cited for contempt for failing to appear. Not coming to court triggered another fine, and failure to pay *that* fine counted as its own form of contempt, adding to the total.

Here, from the DOJ report, is one particularly enraging example of how it all works:

> We spoke, for example, with an African-American woman who has a still-pending case stemming from 2007, when, on a single occasion, she parked her car illegally. She received two citations and a $151 fine, plus fees. The woman, who experienced financial difficulties and periods of homelessness over several years, was charged with seven Failure to Appear offenses for missing court dates or fine payments on her parking tickets between 2007 and 2010. For each Failure to Appear, the court issued an arrest warrant and imposed new fines and fees. From 2007 to 2014, the woman was arrested twice, spent six days in jail, and paid $550 to the court for the events stemming from this single instance of illegal parking. Court records show that she twice attempted to make partial payments of $25 and $50, but the court returned those payments, refusing to accept anything less than payment in full. One of those payments was later accepted, but only after the court's letter rejecting payment by money order was returned as undeliverable. This woman is now making regular payments on the fine. As of December 2014, over seven years later, despite initially owing a $151 fine and having already paid $550, she still owed $541.

By 2015, fines and fees would make up more than one-fifth of the city of Ferguson's total revenue. The local leadership class clearly saw tickets and citations as a convenient source of cash that would fill the city's treasury without their having to do the politically difficult work of raising taxes. The problem with raising, say, property taxes is that the most engaged, empowered citizens will revolt against it. So instead, why not just squeeze all you can out of a smaller, less powerful group of citizens by raising the revenue through enforcement? The citizens receive municipal services, and the subjects have to pay for them. King George III succumbed to the same temptation.

Of course, just as with the colonial customs officers, a policing regime designed to extract revenue and stamp out petty, nonviolent offenses is going to need ever-grander grants of power. The British Crown issued formal writs of assistance that allowed anyone to be searched at any time. The Ferguson police department used its expansive municipal code for the same ends. In addition to the "failure to comply" statute so abused by Ferguson cops (as I discussed earlier), cops could marshal a bevy of other municipal infractions—such as "manner of walking in roadway" violations—for their purposes.

This meant that the black citizens of Ferguson lived in a different country than their white neighbors. They lived in a country without a Fourth Amendment, without the fundamental right to privacy, the right to be "secure" in one's personal effects, whether in one's body, house, or car.

They lived (and continue to live) the contingent existence of the occupied. And here's what that looks like (again, an incident recorded in the DOJ report):

Lieutenant: Get over here. Get the f*** over here.

Man at bus stop: Me?

Lieutenant: Yeah, you.

Man at bus stop: Why? What did I do?

Lieutenant: Give me your ID.

Man at bus stop: Why?

Lieutenant: Stop being a smart ass and give me your ID.

All this was the context for what happened in Ferguson after Michael Brown was killed. I've never been anywhere in the United States that felt as *revolutionary* as those days of unrest in Ferguson. And it wasn't primarily because of the protesters or the relatively small handful of (mostly) young men looting and setting things on fire. It was because the response of the cops was so heavy-handed, so panicky. In response to the outrage that poured forth on that summer afternoon, the police of Ferguson and St. Louis County mobilized as if for war: flak jackets, masks, helmets, camouflage, assault weapons, and armored vehicles. Men pointed their long guns at civilians who assembled for peaceful protest. Cops arrested and detained journalists who were charging their phones in a McDonald's. They fired tear gas canisters indiscriminately. Bands of armed cops in full combat gear chased unarmed, peaceful protesters through the streets with guns raised.

Presented with a challenge to its power, an illegitimate regime will often overreact, driven by the knowledge that all they have is force. As Frantz Fanon wrote in 1961 about French colonialism, "In the colonies, the official, legitimate agent, the spokesperson for the colonizer and the regime of oppression, is the police officer or the soldier. . . . The government's agent uses a language of pure violence. The agent does not alleviate oppression or mask domination. He displays and demonstrates them with the clear conscience of the law enforcer, and brings violence into the homes and minds of the colonized subject."

On the streets of Ferguson, one could, in every moment, feel the police officers' lack of legitimacy. There was nothing behind them; their guns provided their only authority. One threatened to Mace me on live TV because I drifted too close to him while broadcasting. And in his contorted face I could see how terrified he was.

There was one detail of Michael Brown's death that protesters and residents alike kept returning to, and it wasn't the "hands up" contention. It was the body. After the shooting, Michael Brown's body lay in the street for more than four hours: bloody, baking in the hot August sun. His brains spattered on the concrete. Police would say they needed to be diligent with their forensic investigation, but to those who assembled in the minutes after Brown's death, the inert, uncovered, *disrespected* body was the perfect symbol of the Ferguson police's contempt. One resident who was there said it felt like the kind of thing the Mafia would do after a hit—just leave the body out for all to see as a warning—"or one of those cartels down in Mexico. Don't they do that sometimes, kill someone and just leave him out like that?"

To desecrate the dead is to humiliate the living, and humiliation may be the most powerful and most underappreciated force in human affairs. The angry citizen can shout, and the terrified citizen can lock the doors, or flee, or move, or arm himself. But the humiliated citizen can neither express her feelings nor respond to the offense. For it is in the nature of humiliation that it happens at the hands of someone with greater power: the police officer who pulls over the young black man behind the wheel and wants to hear no lip; the corrupt bureaucrat who comes to inspect the businessman's shop, looking for violations; the surly immigration official who goes through the immigrant's belongings.

In Ferguson people were enraged at Michael Brown's death and grieving at his passing, but more than anything else they were sick and tired of being humiliated. At random I could take my microphone and offer it to a black Ferguson resident, young or old, who had a story of being harassed and humiliated. A young honors student and aspiring future politician told me about watching his mother be pulled over and barked at by police. The local state senator told me that when she was a teenager, a police officer drew a gun on her because she was sitting in a fire truck—at a fireman's invitation. At any given moment a black citizen of Ferguson might find himself shown up, dressed down, made to stoop and cower by the men with badges. Another anecdote from the DOJ report shows just how extreme the humiliation could be:

> In the summer of 2012, a 32-year-old African-American man sat in his car cooling off after playing basketball in a Ferguson public park. An officer pulled up behind the man's car, blocking him in, and demanded the man's Social Security number and identification. Without any cause, the officer accused the man of being a pedophile, referring to the presence of children in the park, and ordered the man out of his car for a pat-down, although the officer had no reason to believe the man was armed. The officer also asked to search the man's car. The man objected, citing his constitutional rights. In response, the officer arrested the man, reportedly at gunpoint, charging him with eight violations of Ferguson's municipal code. One charge, Making a False Declaration, was for initially providing the short form of his first name (e.g., "Mike" instead of "Michael"), and an address which, although legitimate, was different from the one on his driver's license. Another charge was for not wearing a seat belt, even though he was seated in a parked car. The officer also charged the man both with having an expired operator's license, and with having no operator's license in his possession. The man told us that, because of these charges, he lost his job as a contractor with the federal government that he had held for years.

Take just a moment to put yourself in that man's position. You are sitting in your own car, minding your own business, and the next thing you know, a cop has accused you of being a child molester, pulled a gun on you, arrested you (for a series of *ridiculous* offenses), and thrown you in jail. For good measure, you've now lost your job.

We can all access some version of this feeling—even people of tremendous privilege can know the sting of humiliation. Take the simple example of a parking ticket. Just about everyone's gotten one. You've been pulled over, and even if it's completely justified, the sight of the cop or traffic agent scribbling on that flipbook causes a flood of neurochemicals. You experience a feeling of injustice, rage, and self-pity at the sheer unfairness of it all. And all this just for a parking ticket! A small citation and an entirely proper acknowledgment that someone, in his or her own small, innocuous, but irrefutable way, broke the law.

FOR SUBJECTS OF AUTHORITARIAN rule, humiliation is the permanent state of existence. "There is the man at the top," Frantz Fanon wrote of his native Martinique, "and there are his courtiers, the indifferent (who are waiting), and the humiliated." That's it. In a colonial system, you can have power and be close to those with power, or you can be humiliated.

It was a sense of profound humiliation that gave emotional fuel to our own revolution. The humiliation that Britain visited upon the American colonists created such a powerful thirst for vengeance, it could be quenched only with extreme acts of ritualized public violence that tried to turn humiliation back on the oppressors. In 1769 a British customs officer named James Rowe was offered a bribe to look the other way as some goods were smuggled. He declined and chose to enforce the law, seizing the black market goods. "In response he was tarred and feathered, wheeled around the town in a cart, and forced to wear signs labeling him an informer."

This happened in Salem, Massachusetts, a town that already knew a thing or two about rituals of public humiliation, but in the run-up to the Revolution, as the Crown attempted to crack down on smuggling, these outbursts of violent mob humiliation became routine. In Newburyport, a customs official was "put in the stocks, then paraded through town with a rope around his neck, hit with eggs, and locked in a warehouse over a weekend before being released." In these moments the colonists could purge their own sense of impotence and transfer it to the agents of the Crown who had imposed it on them. Two centuries later Fanon would say that "colonialism is not a thinking machine, nor a body endowed with reasoning faculties. It is violence in its natural state, and it will only yield when confronted with greater violence."

To the Founders, the solution to the excesses of the Crown was revolution, then a republic. Of course, in the tortured and prolonged negotiations that ultimately created the Constitution, many of the original grievances—particularly the unreasonable searches and seizures, the lack of due process, and the heavy-handed quartering of soldiers in colonists' homes—went unaddressed. Constitutional scholar Akhil Amar says that as soon as the final Constitution made its way out into the states to be debated and ratified, these omissions were immediately evident to the citizens engaged in the debate. Final ratification came only after they were assured that a Bill of Rights, which explicitly addressed many of the Crown's egregious overreaches, was on its way. The framers thus included in the Fourth Amendment these words:

> The right of the people to be secure in their persons, houses, papers, and effects, against unreasonable searches and seizures, shall not be violated, and no Warrants shall issue, but upon probable cause, supported by Oath or affirmation, and particularly describing the place to be searched, and the persons or things to be seized.

The existence of the Bill of Rights is an acknowledgment of the fact that democracy, by itself, is no guarantee against the potential excesses of the state's police power. But on the ground in Ferguson, the Bill of Rights *itself* seemed to have no force. So the question that kept tugging at me, amid the tear gas and the sonic cannon, the shouts and protests and fires, was: What exactly was the "the law" in this heretofore little-known town? Whose authority held here, and why? Was it covered by the Constitution, or had we all managed to slip into some legal multiverse, where the standard rules, the ones our forefathers had fought and died for, that we pledged allegiance to as school children, simply did not exist?

As the DOJ report makes clear, the violations of the Constitution in Ferguson were extreme and systematic. Repeatedly, it calls the Ferguson police department's patterns and practices "unconstitutional," citing various amendments, from the Fourth to the Fifth, Eighth, and Fourteenth, that are habitually violated by the conveyor belt of tickets, citations, court dates, fees, and warrants.

But perhaps the most remarkable aspect of the DOJ report is how open and honest the city officials are about their police department's purpose, how certain they seem that no one is watching them. Their comments suggest no winking and nudging, as one might find in the e-mails of, say, bankers on the eve of the housing crash or Enron traders before the bankruptcy. No ironic and knowing smiles. Just plain statements of financial goals, of dollars and cents. At one point the department started a new "I-270 traffic enforcement initiative" in order to "begin to fill the revenue pipeline." The masterminds behind it warned that the initiative would require "60 to 90 [days] of lead time to turn citations into cash."

The point is that none of the people administering this enterprise appear concerned that what they're doing is a gross violation of their duty to their constituents. And when you ask yourself how this report came to be written, the reason for their nonchalance is evident. The damning pages of the report exist only because a seventeen-year-old black boy was shot and killed by a police officer, and because that shooting led to an uprising. That uprising in turn led to the DOJ getting involved, which in turn led to the investigation that produced this audit.

But how many other police departments are like the one in Ferguson? We happen to know of this one because of this young man's death, because of the outrage and activism and klieg lights that followed that death. But Ferguson's practices were hiding in plain sight for all to see for years. And in fact, when I talked to people in Ferguson, they didn't think there was much that special about it. Go to any of the surrounding little municipalities *around* Ferguson in St. Louis County: Jennings, Florissant, Kinloch. A *Washington Post* investigation of the municipal court system in the our rounding towns found identical violations across the board.

This is what "the law" looks like in the Colony, where real democratic accountability is lacking, when the consent of the governed is absent or forsaken or betrayed, and when the *purpose* of policing and courts isn't the maintenance of safety and provision of justice but rather some other aim. In north St. Louis County that aim is to produce revenue, the same aim of the British Empire's customs regime in the American colonies.

But empires of old kept their colonies at a distance: Rome conquered the Gauls across the Alps. France ruled Algeria from across the Mediterranean. King George III dispatched troops across the Atlantic to administer the new world. In the United States in 2016 such distance does not exist: the "rough" part of Ferguson is maybe a thousand yards from the "nice" neighborhoods.

And so the maintenance of the Nation's integrity requires constant vigilance. The borders must be enforced without the benefit of actual walls and checkpoints. This requires an ungodly number of interactions between the sentries of the state and those the state views as the disorderly class. The math of large numbers means that with enough of these interactions and enough fear and suspicion on the part of the officers who wield the gun, hundreds of those who've been marked for monitoring will die.

One of those deaths was a Staten Island grandfather named Eric Garner, who was choked to death by a New York cop in July 2014. In a small working-class neighborhood in Staten Island, Garner would sell individual cigarettes—loosies—which are illegal in New York.

In other words: Eric Garner, like John Hancock, was a merchant trafficking in black market goods. He was offering what the market demanded—a cheaper, unbundled, untaxed cigarette. And the government seeking to crack down on this offense harassed him—he'd been arrested twice for selling loosies in 2014 alone. Day after day Eric Garner simply had to swallow a particular type of ritualized humiliation. He had to take it. Every day the humiliation and frustration built within him.

On the day he died, Eric Garner was wrestled to the ground and put into a chokehold as he screamed with increasing desperation, "I can't breathe," eleven times, until he lost consciousness and died. All this was recorded as plain as day on a smartphone, which, before the police officer placed Garner in a chokehold, had captured his final protests:

> Every time you see me, you want to mess with me. I'm tired of it. It stops today. . . . Every time you see me, you want to harass me. You want to stop me [*garbled*] selling cigarettes. I'm minding my business, officer, I'm minding my business. Please just leave me alone. I told you the last time, please just leave me alone. Please please, don't touch me. Do not touch me.

Those final words could have been just as well addressed to a colonial customs officer:

Every time you see me, you want to harass me.
It stops today.

J ust after Cleveland police officer Timothy Loehmann fired his sidearm from the passenger side of a police cruiser, his partner Frank Garmback radioed dispatch. The neighborhood that the two officers were patrolling was, from the perspective of two white cops, poor, black, and violent. The park to which they had been summoned with word of a possible active shooter contains a memorial to two other police officers who'd been killed there in the line of duty.

"Shots fired," Garmback told dispatch. "Male down, black male, maybe twenty."

Maybe twenty. Perhaps a few years younger: eighteen, say. Or older: twenty-three. We do not know at what point it was revealed to them that Tamir Rice, whom Loehmann killed with two shots within two seconds of arriving on the scene, was, in fact, only twelve years old. He was not a man with a pistol. He was a boy with a pellet gun.

Loehmann would tell investigators he had had no choice: he saw Rice reach for his waistband and thought he was about to pull out a gun and shoot him. Loehmann wasn't charged. He told the grand jury he was scared, and the grand jury believed him, as did the Cuyahoga County prosecutor who explained the decision: "Believing he was about to be shot was a mistaken—yet reasonable— belief given the high-stress circumstances and his police training. He had reason to fear for his life."

"WAR ZONE" IS THE cliché people tend to reach for when describing poor urban neighborhoods. Various representations of the Bronx in 1980s, like the films *The Warriors* and *Fort Apache: The Bronx* played up this metaphor. In popular culture at the time, my home borough might as well have been Beirut. People constantly used the phrase "bombed out."

This is a common way of understanding urban environments. Not long before Timothy Loehmann shot and killed Tamir Rice, the Department of Justice issued a scathing report on the Cleveland police department's patterns and practices of discrimination and the use of force. One detail sums up the entire problem with the mindset of policing in the Colony. The DOJ had "observed a large sign hanging in the vehicle bay of a district station identifying it as a 'forward operating base,' a military term for 'a small, secured outpost used to support tactical operations in a war zone.'"

Forward operating base. That phrase captures the psychology of many police officers: they see themselves as combatants in a war zone, besieged and surrounded, operating in enemy territory, one wrong move away from sudden death. And here's the thing. It's not an act. I'm sure Timothy Loehmann was indeed terrified. That fear, the fear of the occupying solider, is the entire problem.

The mindset of the occupier in restive and dangerous territory is not unique to the Cleveland police department, of course. Nor is the mindset that led to the death of Tamir Rice new. More than fifty years ago, before the war on drugs, before SWAT teams and mandatory minimums and private prisons and "stop and frisk," before the entire modern-day Colony was constructed, James Baldwin wrote that a white police officer "moves through Harlem . . . like an occupying soldier in a bitterly hostile country."

If the white Harlem cop in Baldwin's day walked the streets stalked by fear of the natives, aware he was fundamentally foreign to the land he patrolled, then he was partaking in an American tradition that stretches back, in a literal way, to the country's origins.

To be outnumbered and afraid in a land not your own, and to attempt to bring it under your control—this is the great recurring theme of the American project, and it is shot through at every moment by fear and violence and subjugation. That fear stalks our history's winners even as they conquer and conquer and settle and conquer some more.

The first European settlers who arrived in Jamestown were attacked almost immediately. The early colonial governor of Virginia George Percy, who helped sail the Virginia Company of London's first fleet, recalled the first day of landfall in 1606.

> At night, when we were going aboard, there came the Savages creeping upon all fours, from the Hills, like Bears, with their Bows in their mouths, [who] charged us very desperately in the faces, hurt Captain Gabriel Archer in both his hands, and a sailor in two places of the body very dangerous. After they had spent their Arrows, and felt the sharpness of our shot, they retired into the Woods with a great noise, and so left us.

The experience of Jamestown was dire and miserable, a tale of violence, sickness, death, and ultimately abandonment. Six hundred miles north in Plymouth, things wouldn't be quite as bad, but despite our Thanksgiving myth of peaceable coexistence, fear cloaked life in its every instant. The relationship between settlers and Indians mostly consisted of mutual terror punctuated by atrocities. Squanto, the lovable English-speaking Indian of the Thanksgiving story, was actually a man who'd been kidnapped from his village, then transported across the Atlantic to be sold into slavery in Europe. He would escape and make it back to America only to find out his entire village had been wiped out by European disease.

The Thanksgiving tradition we celebrate today with a feast actually commemorates a betrayal that happened two years after the first arrival of the colonists. In 1622, Myles Standish, an English military officer working for the Pilgrims, heard that Indians planned to raid the newly established white settlement of Wessagussett. Standish organized a militia to repel the attack, but no Indians appeared. So he decided to preemptively attack by luring two Indians to Wessagussett under the pretense of sharing a meal. When they entered the house, Standish and his men killed them.

Bernard Bailyn, the great scholar of the American colonial project's first century, calls this period the "barbarous years." "The savagery," he once wrote, was driven by "elemental fears peculiar to what was experienced as a barbarous environment—fears of what could happen to civilized people in an unimaginable wilderness . . . in which God's children," as the colonists thought of themselves, "were fated to struggle with pitiless agents of Satan, pagan Antichrists swarming in the world around them."

Within a century or two, settlers and the U.S. government had succeeded in ethnically cleansing, conquering, and corralling the continent's indigenous people. But there would always be a new enemy at the gate. In the South, of course, it was the constant demographic weight of the slaves under the whip, who so outnumbered their masters that the possibility of revolt dominated the nightmares of the slaver class. The master went to bed in his house every night, protected from dozens of men and women he owned by his accumulated weaponry and his ability to terrorize them.

Revolts happened often enough that southern planters didn't have to simply imagine what would happen if the scales were to suddenly tip. In 1770 the *Virginia Gazette* carried an account of a slave revolt in Bowler Cocke's Hanover County plantation, indicating the cause: "The Negroes belonging to the plantation having long been treated with too much lenity and indulgence, were grown extremely insolent and unruly." Ultimately a group of about a dozen white men (and two children bearing weapons) confronted the forty or fifty slaves armed with nothing but farm tools:

> The slaves, deaf to all they said, rushed upon them with desperate fury, armed with clubs and staves; one of them knocked down a White man, and was going to repeat the blow to finish him, which one of the boys seeing, levelled his piece, discharged its contents into the fellow's breast, and brought him to the dust. Another fellow, having also knocked down another of the Whites, was, in the same manner, shot by the other boy. In short, the battle continued sometime desperate, but another of the Negroes having his head almost cut off with a broad sword, and five of them being wounded, the rest fled.

Fear, of course, is not all that motivates the settler, the col-onizer, the slaveowner. Another inducement, as Ta-Nehisi Coates says, is "plunder." But the existence of plunder as a motivation, even as the primary one, does not negate the subjective experience of white fear, the terror that individ-ual white people experience and that white writers, preach-ers, and politicians cultivate socially and politically. That dispatch in the *Virginia Gazette* was meant to terrify those who read it, and I'm certain it succeeded.

It may seem downright perverse to linger on this kind of fear, the fear felt by enslavers and white colonists. If we point to the fear that motivates a lynch mob, then what are we saying about the moral status of the murder they all com-mitted? Does their fear justify it? The obvious answer is no. The slaves had infinitely more to fear than the slaveowners, and the Indians had infinitely more to fear than the settlers. Even to diagnose and investigate white fear in this period seems an injustice: the fear that should matter to us is the fear of the man who has been murdered, the fear felt by his family and kin and friends and the millions of African Americans across the South who lived through decades of systematic terrorism with essentially no protection from the state. When we think of fear and the lynch mob, we should of course think of the victim, not of the crowd.

But for the Pilgrim in the land of the pagans, the home-steader scratching out a bare existence for a terrified fam-ily just a day's ride from Comanches, the planter patriarch whose family sleeps outnumbered every night, fear is not some *excuse for* savagery, cruelty, and sadism but is fundamentally inseparable from it. Hurt people hurt people, as the old saying goes. And the truly terrified commit atrocities.

Ultimately the gun is the backstop that prevents the entire social order from being upended. Had it not been for the superior firepower of fearful whites, who knows what would have transpired in American history? You can understand why, in such a situation, certain kinds of white southerners would cling to their guns.

Today Americans still rely on the gun, the power to kill or injure, to preserve the social order in the most fraught and dire moments. Police know their weapon is by their side if the situation they encounter spins too far out of control and they find themselves threatened.

OF COURSE, THE OVERWHELMING majority of police interactions never go near this danger zone. A huge number of calls that come into 911 are complaints not of violent threats but about simple disorder: unruly people on the street, loud music coming from apartment parties, interpersonal conflict teetering on the edge of violence, like the argument that started this book. While law enforcement likes to urge vigilance—if you see something, say something—sometimes, particularly in rapidly gentrifying areas, this ends up being something of a constant headache for police.

"So I'm working last week and get dispatched to a call of 'Suspicious Activity,'" reads a post on Reddit's police message board ProtectAndServe.

> Ya'll wanna know what the suspicious activity was? Someone walking around in the dark with a flashlight and crow bar? Nope. Someone walking into a bank with a full face mask on? Nope. It was two black males who were jump starting a car at 930 in the morning. That was it. Nothing else. Someone called it in.

In the course of the last few years, I've had dozens and dozens of conversations with cops, but I'm always struck that for all the training and procedures that accompany being a member of a police force, each police officer has a shocking amount of latitude in any given situation. When I read the above Reddit post, I feel relief that the cop who answered the call to find two guys jumping their car had the good sense not to harass them. But who knows what another cop would've done?

At the street level, that autonomy is both an essential part of policing and the source of what so many people in the Colony find so maddening and humiliating. From the cops' perspective, anything can happen in any interaction—they need the latitude to manage and control whatever they encounter. But for two young black men trying to jump-start a car, no doubt frustrated and late for work, the arrival of a police officer is the arrival of a government agent who may be in a beneficent mood or in a vengeful one. In the moment of his appearance, they go from sovereign to second-class citizens.

To better understand how cops learn to wield this authority, I traveled to New Jersey, to spend a morning in the Morris County Sheriff's Office. I wanted to experience firsthand how recruits are trained to navigate the irreducible uncertainty of being out on the street in the office's state-of-the-art virtual reality simulator.

I am standing in the center of a dark, circular room almost entirely surrounded by screens. I am outfitted with a receptor on my chest that can receive gunshots fired from actors playing roles on the screens in front of me. When I am hit, I will feel a shock. I have a nine-millimeter handgun that has been converted to fire an infrared signal at the simulator screens but retains its original action and noise.

At the controls behind me stands Paul Carifi. A bald and jacked forty-nine-year-old white man with the compact intensity of a human bulldog, he's been overseeing training for years. I cannot conjure in my mind someone who's more of a cop's cop. Later I will learn he's also a Republican member of the Parsippany town council.

On the computer system, he can pull up any one of eighty-five different scenarios and then manipulate it in real time as I interact with the scene in front of me. Actors on a video screen will speak to me. They will appear to respond to my commands, though really it's Carifi making dynamic selections from a menu of responses available on the computer. Each scenario begins with a call from dispatch giving me some cursory information about what I'm being summoned to, and then a few moments later, there I am confronting the scene alone.

"So you want to maintain control, some semblance of order," Carifi tells me before I start. "You want [your suspects] to stay in one spot. You want their hands out where you can see their hands. You don't want people moving around, sticking their hands in their pockets, in their jackets, because now you don't know what they're grabbing for. . . . You want to be able to maintain a calmness, so when you're talking to people you're not getting upset, getting riled up. And if they are, you want to calm them down."

In the first scenario I happen upon, a white man, probably in his late fifties, is standing in the back of a pickup truck, throwing junk from his flatbed into an empty lot. He's not hurting anyone. There's no one else around, but what he's doing is a clear violation of the law, and I have to get him to stop. I don't know what law he's violating, and I have a sneaking suspicion that a rookie cop might not either.

I summon my best commanding voice and ask the man on the screen before me what he's doing.

"Great," he says. "I knew someone was gonna call you guys."

"Yeah, uh, what are you up to here?"

"Why you gotta give me a hard time?"

"Well, this is not a dumping ground." I don't actually know if that's true. But would a real cop in my position who just showed up know the ins and outs of dumping laws?

"This is my friend's lot. I can dump here."

Again: maybe true! Who knows? I press on. "Uh, no. I'm going to have to ask you to pack up your stuff and go."

"My friend owns this property."

"You got any proof?"

"Shut up, you dumbass."

I freeze for a moment. Obviously, I can't let this dude call me a dumbass and tell me to shut up. But what exactly is my recourse? I mean, I suppose I could try to slap some cuffs on him for disorderly conduct or resisting arrest. Instead I say, "Uh."

"Relax, man. It's only a little fucking concrete. It ain't gonna kill ya." He holds a cinder block in his hands.

"Okay, can you drop that please for me?" I attempt to affect a voice of authority, even though I'm asking a question. Which I probably shouldn't do. And then just to make sure he understands which precise implement I'm asking him to drop, I add, "That concrete block."

"You want me to put the block down?"

"Yeah. Yes, sir."

"Put the block down. Yeah, I'll put the block down." At that point he raises the cinder block above his head as if to throw at me.

I respond by drawing my weapon and aiming it at him.

The simulation ends.

Carifi asks me if I was right to draw my weapon, and the obvious embarrassing answer is no, of course not. The man is far enough away that he can't really hit me with a cinder block. This, of course, delights Carifi. We're only one scene in, and already the self-righteous liberal pundit has drawn his weapon on an unarmed man holding a cinder block.

"I probably didn't need to go to my gun," I say somewhat sheepishly.

"You don't. You see that especially with some of our newer trainees. They want to go to the gun right away."

For Carifi, and for the good folks of New Jersey law enforcement and beyond, this is already mission accomplished. Police officers dislike being second-guessed by politicians, activists, and journalists who've never had to do their job, and in this context the exercise is designed to beat some humility into loudmouth pundits like myself. See—it's not so easy, right?

We continue to another scenario: a pimp yelling at and verbally threatening a sex worker who seems strung out. The pimp tells me to scram, and when I hold my ground, he takes off. I stay behind to help the sex worker, who briefly threatens to stab me with a hypodermic needle, but I don't take the bait this time. My weapon stays holstered, and she ultimately puts the syringe down.

In the next scenarios, I pull over a group of kids who look stoned out of their gourd blasting metal in a car in the parking lot of a mall; confront a couple whose neighbors have called in a noise complaint about music blasting from a garage; and enter a chaotic scene at a suburban home in which a man's ex-girlfriend has parked her SUV in front of his driveway. She's yelling at him and refusing to let him and his new girlfriend leave.

I do my best through all of them, but I keep coming back to ask how much training I would want to have in order to feel prepared to intervene confidently and appropriately in some of the situations I encounter in the simulator. I imagine cops have to mediate between exes having loud confrontations all the time, and I also imagine that, say, someone with years of conflict resolution and psychological training would have a pretty clear road map for how to best resolve a situation like that without having to make an arrest, use pepper spray, or god forbid, unholster his weapon.

"There's an old saying," retired NYPD cop turned author Steve Osborne once told me, "that in police work, a cop's mouth is his greatest weapon. To go into a chaotic situation where everybody is yelling and screaming, sometimes there's alcohol, there's drugs involved—to be able to talk everybody down. When you see a real experienced cop do that, it's a magical thing."

But as true as that is, the fact is that most cops are going to encounter these scenarios with little more training than I did—and I talk for a living! The typical cadet training involves sixty hours on how to use a gun and fifty-one hours on defensive tactics, but just eight hours on how to calm situations without force.

It made me think of the stories I'd heard from soldiers about the high-water mark of counterinsurgency in Iraq, when General David Petraeus (to much acclaim) took over the mission. He attempted to orient America's occupying soldiers toward cultivating political alliances and building the new state's governing capacity. Readers of American news outlets were treated to an endless stream of photos of camo-clad soldiers sitting on rugs with Iraqi men drinking tea and listening to them air their grievances.

Some of the soldiers I spoke to enjoyed this work, believed in it deeply, and felt they excelled at it. Others felt the whole thing was ridiculous. But the brute fact remains: soldiers aren't judges or mayors or bureaucrats who have the experience, language skills, or basic relationships of kin and country to be able to navigate the extremely fraught local politics of a place they've never set foot in until their deployment.

Sure, there were many incredibly talented, humane, creative American troops who managed to improvise, listen and learn, and play some kind of constructive role in the area to which they were assigned. But there was a fundamental mismatch between what the military as an institution is created and trained to do and what this military in this moment was being asked to do. The military exists to use violence to destroy enemies. That is its essence. It can also do many things that aren't that (build dams, deliver relief, develop technology), but to ask twenty-year-olds in a war zone to play cultural ambassador underneath fifty pounds of gear in 110-degree heat while not speaking the language is, well, a stretch.

And as I navigated scenario after scenario in the training room, it felt like it's in many ways the same for cops. We ask police to be social workers, addiction counselors, mental health workers, and community mediators. We wouldn't hand a social worker a gun and have them go out into the streets to apprehend criminals, but we do the opposite every day.

So what happens when police officers are called upon to handle a volatile person in the midst of terrible psychological torment? It happens all the time in America, and many police, whether through luck or accrued wisdom or basic empathy, handle it with grace. But many don't, or worse. In March 2015 a maintenance worker in an apartment complex in the Atlanta suburbs saw twenty-seven-year-old Air Force veteran Anthony Hill naked, banging on neighbors' doors and crawling on the ground in the throes of a bipolar episode. The worker did what many, maybe most, of us would do: he called the cops. What else would you do? This is precisely the type of disorder we look to the cops to resolve. (Another woman who saw Hill called 911, hoping to get medical personnel to respond.)

The police arrived, and in less than ten minutes, Hill, who was black, was shot dead. He had been unarmed and, his family says, suffered from PTSD after a deployment to Afghanistan. The officer who shot him claimed that Hill charged him, and he was convinced he was on some drug that would've rendered his Taser useless. That officer was charged with murder.

But take a second and ask yourself why this was considered something for the police to handle to begin with. "If a mental health unit with paramedics, nurses, or even doctors had been sent to help Anthony (instead of an officer with a gun) he would still be alive today," local activist Asia

Parks told *Think Progress*. "Mental illness should not be the reason a person is condemned to death or prison." According to statistics compiled by the *Washington Post*, in 2015 a full quarter of those shot and killed by police were suffering from mental illness.

None of my scenarios in New Jersey involved people suffering from mental illness, although I was hardly in a position to make that determination. (Again: how would I know unless I had been trained to spot it?) One simulation stuck out, however, probably because it ended with me getting shot.

I show up in response to a complaint that a man is revving the engine of his motorcycle in his garage. When I ask about the noise, the man stops revving the engine and responds, "Are you kidding me? Are you fucking kidding me! Again?!" I stand in the driveway looking into the garage, where the man and his wife take turns arguing with each other and cursing at me. I try to control the situation, but after maybe thirty seconds of this kind of back-and-forth, the man and the woman start arguing more strenuously. Then suddenly, someone starts firing a shotgun at me. I am hit before my hand even reaches my sidearm. Despite being shot, I manage to draw my gun and fire wildly, but by that point I am (virtually) dead.

Carifi approached me and asked me how many people were in the scenario. I said two, the man and woman arguing. I had managed to entirely miss a third man who'd entered the scene and been the one to pick up the shotgun. To add insult to injury, he noted the screen that marked where I had returned fire: my constellation of misses hadn't even come close to the man actually trying to kill me.

"Your shots were all over the place," Carifi said. "The scenario ended at this point because he got off multiple shots with his shotgun. Most likely you're—"

"Toast," I said.

"—in trouble," Carifi said diplomatically. "Now on this particular scenario," he continued, "this might happen a hundred thousand times. The people will listen to you, and it will end calmly. But it's that one out of every hundred thousand, two hundred thousand calls that this happens."

And there's the nub of it. Let's imagine you're watching two men argue loudly in the middle of a street. It's tense and uncomfortable. You might call the cops in hopes of making sure it doesn't escalate. This isn't an everyday occurrence (though it depends on where you live), but it's routine enough that it presents no great crisis. I've witnessed such scenes in numerous countries, particularly in Italy, where loud, performative arguments on the street happen as a matter of course. In that context, no one so much as bats an eye, let alone calls the cops, unless punches are thrown. People argue loudly sometimes! That is not the case in the United States, where loud public arguments, indeed any displays of disorderliness, often carry more than a wisp of genuine danger, because you never know if the hothead who cut you off in traffic, or the drunk in the booth next to you at the bar, might be packing.

Policing in an environment awash in guns is fundamen-

tally different from policing in one that isn't. In every interaction in the simulator, I wondered when the gun would
appear, and when I'd find myself reaching for my holster.
Obviously the training environment and the desire to
expose me to as much "action" as possible exaggerated the
fear of the ever-present gun.

But afterward, in a conversation with former cops, they all
told me the threat of the gun weighs heavily. Over his years
as a cop and a supervisor, Steve Osborne told me,

> I was involved in literally thousands of arrests. And
> everything goes smooth, everything goes smooth, it
> goes smooth. For me, it was when I least expected it,
> I had little to no warning, you go to ring the guy's
> doorbell, there was some Wall Street guy, I went to
> go lock him up, he answered the door with a gun
> and a vest on. Stopped two guys in the street just to
> question them, the guy pulls out a gun for me and
> the next thing I know I'm in a fight for my life so you
> always have to be prepared.

THE SAME SPECTER OF the gun haunted Ferguson. The protests after Michael Brown's shooting were almost entirely
nonviolent. Chaotic, sometimes. Boisterous, aggressive, and
profane. But the through line for most of them was that the
protesters seemed in much more danger than the police.

The police had guns, which occasionally they would take out and aim at protesters. The protesters had, at most, glass bottles to launch at the cops in their riot gear. On the long nights that would inevitably end in tear gas, as the standoffs grew tenser, and as disorder beckoned, my own anxiety centered on the possibility that we were just one hotheaded cop away from another dead body.

But on the cold night in November 2014 when St. Louis County state's attorney Bob McCullough announced the grand jury's finding for Officer Darren Wilson, it was a very different scene. We arrived at a protest outside the Ferguson police headquarters an hour or so after McCullough announced that no one would be prosecuted for Michael Brown's death. There was more than a bite of menace in the air. Young men stalking around with their faces covered. Children, families, and elders who had been mainstays at earlier protests seemed noticeably absent, or they headed away as they sensed trouble was about to start. In the several-block walk from where we parked the car to the street outside the police headquarters, I thought I heard the faint sound of gunfire but convinced myself someone was just setting off firecrackers.

We stood across the street from the headquarters, where a single squad car was parked in an otherwise empty parking lot. About a dozen cops in full riot gear stood in front of the car, impassively taking in the scene. Down the block someone started lighting a cop car on fire, and the crowd surged in that direction to watch. Most of the police looked on as well, sensing, it seemed to me, that the odds were not going to be in their favor if they ventured into the streets.

I started down the street to get a closer look at the commotion around the car that was being set on fire (a process that actually takes a while, as I've learned) when I heard a *pop pop pop*. Firecrackers, I thought again, but then I saw the crowd running full tilt toward me, and then I heard the sound again and actually saw the fire coming out of the muzzle of a handgun about forty feet away.

Mayhem and chaos reigned. Onlookers ran in every direction and fell to the ground for cover. We crouched behind the news van positioned at the scene for our live shot (that wasn't going to happen), and I looked across the street. The cops in full riot gear had taken cover behind their lone cruiser. Crouched on the far side of the vehicle, some were peeking up over the hood and scanning for the shooter. They looked like an army squad in a war zone. And they looked legitimately terrified.

We scurried off in the car we'd parked a few blocks away, to the site of the original protests on West Florissant. There we watched as people broke into and looted several of the stores on the block, setting a few of them on fire, including a storage space directly across from us. As we continued to broadcast unfolding events, an air of sadness and rage hung over it all. The block took on the smell of a campfire, as the storage space burned. And while the scene was surreal and chaotic, it didn't feel particularly menacing or dangerous, certainly not the way those gunshots had. Then late in the night, a burst of automatic gunfire rang out just fifty yards away and sent us scurrying indoors.

How darkly magical is the presence of the gun! How remarkable its power to transform the order of things. The scene without the gun had been chaotic, boisterous, and angry, while the one with the gun was dangerous, panicked, and flight-inducing. They existed in two parallel dimensions, and at the first crack of gunfire, we warped from one to the other.

Amid the adrenaline, I felt an acute stab of empathy for those police officers huddled by the cruiser earlier in the night, and then for every cop who moves through this country of ours where there is more than one gun for every man, woman, and child. I saw just for the briefest of instants, with my nose pressed to the pavement beneath the news van, the way the presence of guns, their easy concealability and ubiquity, transforms the very essence of disorder. For those tasked with enforcing the state's authority, unruliness is uncomfortable. Cops don't like it anywhere. And cops in any society clash with protesters and use all kinds of tactics, some rough, others less so, to suppress and disperse them.

Many other wealthy democracies have traditions of far more robust street protest than we have in the United States. When I spent six months living and studying in Bologna, leftist protests complete with Molotov cocktails, riot gear, and tear gas were a relatively frequent occurrence. But the difference in Bologna, and almost everywhere else in

Europe and Asia, is the near total absence of guns. A gun has transformational power.

Sure enough, before very long, Ferguson saw gun violence against the police. In March, a few months after I saw the gunshots and burned cars outside the Ferguson police department, two police officers were shot, one in the face, while policing a protest in that very same spot where they'd taken cover that night. The gunshots were fired by twenty-year-old Jeffrey Williams—it's unclear whether he was a protester. Williams told police the shooting had nothing to do with the protests, saying he fired in self-defense when someone else with whom he had a conflict rolled up on him. Both cops survived, thank god. The five Dallas police officers at a 2016 Black Lives Matter protest murdered by a crazed, anti-cop spree shooter weren't so lucky. Same for the three officers drawn into a deadly ambush that same year in Baton Rouge.

This threat, the threat of the sudden bullet, extends to every single aspect of policing. Japanese police, I'm sure, are summoned to noise complaints all the time, but they arrive at the site without harboring the nagging fear that the interaction will end in gunfire. There simply aren't very many guns in Japan. (Japanese police only began carrying guns in 1946—at the insistence of the American military.) And as rare as it is in the United States for someone during a noise complaint to randomly grab a shotgun and start firing, as happened in my simulation, it's a possibility one must train for.

THE GUN IS PROTECTION and solace. In neighborhoods that are quiet and far from crime and danger, it represents some kind of last personal means of ensuring your own turf. You live in the Nation, and if the Colony comes knocking in the dead of night, you can keep it at bay. In neighborhoods like Freddie Gray's in Westside Baltimore, or in the West Side of Chicago, or in Compton, California, where the state's monopoly on violence is broken or nonexistent, a gun makes a whole heck of a lot of sense. If the law won't protect you, you need to protect yourself.

The Second Amendment, its most strenuous defenders like to tell us, is the ultimate check against tyranny. (This despite the fact that Iraq under Saddam Hussein had one of the highest rates of gun ownership in the world.) They argue that an armed populace repels tyranny, but its practical effect has been the opposite. If the people are armed enough to threaten the state's control, then the state's monopoly on violence is in question, and it therefore often acts less like it's enforcing the law than putting down an insurrection.

An armed populace must be subdued with even greater arms. During the Crack Years, the period in the late 1980s when crack was entering urban America and drug turf wars escalated, mayors in major cities decried the fact that their officers were "outgunned." American society has witnessed a kind of arms race between its citizens and its police, resulting in forces that in many places patrol and occupy rather than police, that straightforwardly view themselves as waging war. "We have a war. We are going to be successful," the Los Angeles police department's infamous Daryl Gates told the press in the late 1980s. "Whatever we need to do to be successful, we will do it."

It was Gates who first created SWAT teams, whose use, as Radley Balko documents in *Rise of the Warrior Cop*, has since exploded. We are now a nation in which SWAT teams armed like special forces in Afghanistan show up at quiet homes in the dark of night, shoot dogs, and terrify residents, all to bust someone for growing pot. And what Seth Stoughton calls the "warrior worldview" has infected law enforcement everywhere. "Under this warrior worldview," he writes, "officers are locked in intermittent and unpredictable combat with unknown but highly lethal enemies."

The more guns are out there, the greater the possibility you, an ordinary citizen, might be on the wrong side of one, a certain line of thinking goes. And so the more it makes sense to be armed yourself. Indeed, after every major mass shooting event, just as sure as the cameras flock to the scene and a national debate about gun violence briefly reemerges, gun sales spike. It turns out that wall-to-wall coverage of people being brutally killed by a gun is the best of all advertisements for gun sales.

A few days after fourteen people were murdered in the December 2015 mass shooting in San Bernardino, I visited a local gun shop run by a former local cop named Mike Wirz. The phone was literally ringing off the hook. "Normally the business increases after things of this nature," he told me between calls. While this particular mass shooting was the closest to home, it wasn't the first high-profile mass murder that had happened in the six years since he retired from San Bernardino sheriff's department and opened his gun shop. The pattern was, he told me, pretty darn consistent. "You see people calling who have never owned a gun in their entire life trying to find out how to purchase a gun, when they can pick it up, when they get one, where they can get training for firearms."

"What is that about?" I asked him.

"Just fear in general."

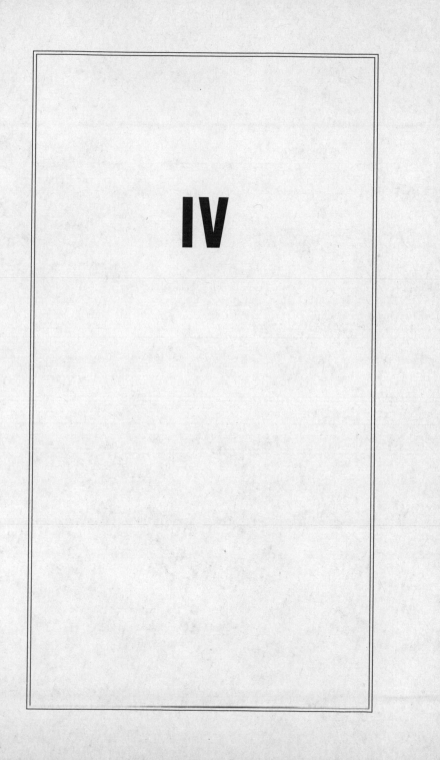

IV

t is more than "fear in general" that maintains the Colony. It is, in fact, a very specific type of fear: white fear.

Despite the fact nonwhite people are disproportion ately the victims of crime, the criminal justice system as a whole is disproportionately built on the emotional foundation of white fear. But then, that isn't surprising. American history is the story of white fear, of the constant violent impulses it produces and the management and ordering of those impulses. White fear keeps the citizens of the Nation wary of the Colony, and fuels their desire to keep it separate.

In fact, I don't think you can really understand why the Colony was built, how America created the largest prison system in the world, without reckoning with the potency of white fear and its deployment. And to illustrate just how pervasive and powerful it is, it's worth taking a little time to play a bit of mass incarceration whodunit.

All things being equal, we'd expect more crime to lead to more people in prison, and indeed, in key periods over the last forty years, the rising levels of crime led to large increases in the prison population. But that is far from the whole story.

Scholars of prisons often talk about the "punishment rate," which is the number of inmates per one thousand reported crimes. It is a useful measure, because it captures how punitive the society is relative to how dangerous it is. Between 1960 and 1980, as the crime rate spiked and the existing system processed the increase, the punishment rate actually fell dramatically. That is, we locked up a relatively small percentage of people compared to the overall number of crimes committed. But starting in 1980, the punishment rate skyrocketed. And then, crucially, even as crime began to fall and then fell sharply in the mid-1990s, the incarceration rate continued to rise. Why did this happen?

Perhaps the most politically fashionable answer at this moment is the War on Drugs. And for good reason: its launch marked a major surge in aggressive, militarized policing. Beginning in the late 1960s and accelerating in the 1980s and 1990s, the federal government expanded its efforts to combat the sale and consumption of illegal drugs. When President Nixon signed the Controlled Substances Act (CSA) in 1970, more than two hundred drug laws were brought under one statute. In 1973 Nixon created, through an executive order, the Drug Enforcement Administration to enforce the CSA, which would grow from a budget of $75 million and 1,470

agents to a budget of over $2 billion and 5,000 agents. The
Reagan administration would later launch an expensive and
expansive propaganda effort to curtail drug use under the
slogan "Just Say No." Reagan's successor, George H. W. Bush,
established a White House Office of National Drug Control
Policy. The number of people in state and federal prisons
serving drug sentences increased nearly 1,270 percent, from
24,000 inmates in 1980 to 304,500 in 2014. Years later Nixon
aide John Ehrlichman seemed to offer up a smoking gun
when he told a reporter:

> The Nixon campaign in 1968, and the Nixon White
> House after that, had two enemies: the antiwar left
> and black people. You understand what I'm saying?
> We knew we couldn't make it illegal to be either
> against the war or black, but by getting the public
> to associate the hippies with marijuana and blacks
> with heroin, and then criminalizing both heavily, we
> could disrupt those communities. We could arrest
> their leaders, raid their homes, break up their meet-
> ings, and vilify them night after night on the evening
> news. Did we know we were lying about the drugs?
> Of course we did.

The federal War on Drugs went hand in hand with a similar push at the local level. In cities across the country, police
departments shifted resources toward drug enforcement. In
1980 the percentage of drug arrests as a proportion of all

arrests in Baltimore was 8 percent. In 2003 it went to 39 percent. In Chicago it rose from 5 percent to 28 percent. In New York it grew from 5 percent to 14 percent.

This unprecedented shift in policy has been rife with obvious, violent, and absurd contradictions. There's strong evidence that white and black people use marijuana at identical rates, and yet black people are four times more likely to be arrested for marijuana possession, and in some states, including Iowa, Minnesota, and Illinois, they are up to eight times as likely to be arrested.

These glaring disparities and racial injustices have rightly focused tremendous energy on ending drug prohibition, a movement that has had striking political success in the last decade. But the War on Drugs accounts for only about 20 percent of the increase in incarceration.

Indeed, in the final years of the Obama administration, many have called on the White House to take the lead in releasing nonviolent drug offenders, who have become the most high-profile category of the incarcerated in political campaigns to reduce imprisonment. But the federal government could release every single nonviolent drug offender currently serving time in a federal prison, and the United States would *still* have the highest incarceration rate in the world.

Activists, reformers, and politicians have also targeted the harshness of criminal sentencing. In 1984 President Reagan signed the Sentencing Reform Act, which established mandatory minimum sentences that constrained judicial discretion. In 1986 Congress passed laws creating a 100-

to-1 sentencing disparity between crack cocaine and pow-
der cocaine. This change was widely understood as racially
biased due to the consumption of crack in poor neighborhoods. It went hand in hand with so-called "truth in sentencing" laws and with parole reforms that vastly curtailed
the eligibility of prisoners for parole, meaning they were far
more likely to serve more of the sentences on the books.

All these increases in sentencing at state and local levels
had a profound effect. Before the Sentencing Reform Act of
1984, the average federal drug offender could expect to serve
58 percent of his sentence, with the remainder on parole.
After 1986 that increased to at least 87 percent. From 1986
to 1997 average federal prison sentences for drug offenders
more than doubled from thirty months to sixty-six months.

But John Pfaff, a law professor and economist at Ford
ham who does empirical work on the causes of mass incarceration, points out that even as incarceration exploded in
the 1990s, median time served has been either flat or in
decline, while the number of arrests for drug law violations
increased from 500,000 in 1982 to 1.5 million in 2007. He
argues that the number of people being thrown into the system (through arrests and prosecutions), not the total time
they spend there, has driven mass incarceration.

For this, Pfaff blames prosecutors, not cops. Prosecutors
have tremendous discretion over which cases to bring and
which to drop, whether to throw the book or slap the wrist.
"You have to focus as much on the culture as the law," he
says. "Prosecutors are part of a culture that has expectations

about crime toughness, and when you combine that with their tremendous amount of latitude, you get staggering punitiveness."

The beat cop deciding to make an arrest, the local district attorney deciding to charge someone with five crimes carrying a max of forty years rather than one with a max of five—these are the individuals who comprise what we call the criminal justice system. But there's no such thing as the criminal justice system. "The criminal justice system is not a 'system' at all," Pfaff writes, "and treating it as such can lead analysts to overlook important causes of prison growth."

American criminal law is constructed, maintained, patrolled, and enforced through a highly distributed, at times byzantine and chaotic set of overlapping jurisdictions, interacting awkwardly with one another. No one takes orders from any unified entity. No single actor or group of actors created mass incarceration, and no single group of actors can undo it. We have no single switch to flip. The Colony is an emergent phenomenon.

There's a deeper story here, about how over the same period of time many different institutional actors all moved in the same direction, namely toward more: more arrests, longer sentences, more aggressive prosecutions, more years before parole, more criminal statutes on the books, more money spent on prisons. The list is endless.

An astounding confluence of thousands of institutions and millions of individuals was necessary to produce the modern American prison state. Think for a moment how hard it is to make major policy changes in America—to shift from fossil fuels to renewable energy, to implement something approximating universal health care. Think of all the special interests and resistance and organizations and constituencies that must be fought, bargained with, steamrolled, cajoled, and bought off. Then think of what it took to create the monstrous expansion of the Colony.

Like a magnet tugging countless tiny filings into the bands of force around its poles, a profoundly powerful political force was at work acting on the thousands of individual systems, actors, and institutions, bringing them into a tyrannical alignment.

That force was white fear.

White fear is both a social fact and something burned into our individual neural pathways. In laboratory studies white people rate children of all races equally "innocent" until about age ten, when the innocence of black children suddenly fades, while that of white children endures. In experimental settings, people of all races perceive black people as more threatening than people of other races, but the effect is particularly exaggerated with white respondents. These studies don't ask respondents for their conscious racial attitudes or articulable political beliefs. Rather, they test respondents in split-second decision making: hitting one button for friend and another for foe, as images of people, black and white, some armed and some carrying groceries, pop up on the screen.

The point of these experiments is to test our deepest,

least conscious, most hardwired reactions to people of different races. Time and time again they uncover that even those with egalitarian racial politics possess unconscious bias. In fact, while white participants have higher levels of racial bias than nonwhite subjects, even African Americans consistently show antiblack suspicion. Racial fear lives in the deepest part of our psyches. It lurks in our synapses.

After every fatal shooting of an unarmed civilian, all actors in the drama follow a familiar script. The police officer in question says he was scared for his life, and public opinion coalesces around either believing him or considering him a liar and a murderer who shot his victim in cold blood. Sometimes a video emerges that supports the latter conclusion: a man fleeing on foot is shot in the back; a young man striding away is hit as an officer unloads a clip of bullets.

In the overwhelming majority of cases, however, no such video exists. And without visual evidence, prosecuting attorneys are inclined to trust the testimony of their colleagues in law enforcement. Grand juries, too, are reluctant to conclude that a cop was lying when he said he feared for his life. In 2008, for example, New York police detective Gescard Isnora testified to a grand jury that he had been "scared and nervous" before he shot eleven of the fifty bullets alongside his unit that killed unarmed New Yorker Sean Bell and wounded two of his friends.

But an officer can suffer fear and still act unjustly. Imagine a police officer in the laboratory, sitting before the psychological test I just mentioned. He is presented with images of men and women, young and old, some aiming a weapon, others cradling a doll, and in a split second he must decide whether to "shoot." And imagine that this particular officer, not through conscious racism but through deep *unconscious* bias, finds himself only in fear of black citizens. In test after test, pictures of black postal workers and teenagers appear on his screen. He hits the "shoot" button over and over again, mistaking for weapons the envelopes and phones in their hands. He is not faking his fear; he is not being disingenuous. But something is deeply amiss.

What is the moral status of that fear? What is its legal status? In the case of a police officer, the practical effect of our collective conception of fear is its transcendent ability to exculpate. If a cop shoots someone because he is angry, he is a murderer. But if he shoots a suspect because he is afraid, he is innocent. Can the law second-guess that subconscious impulse, which the shooter cannot control any more than he can keep his leg from kicking out when a doctor strikes a hammer against his knee?

I KNOW THAT IMPULSE well because I experienced it for much of my life. During my childhood and adolescence, I walked the streets of New York shrouded in white fear, always sensing danger lurking at the corners. The sketchy teenagers up to some kind of hustle in the park. The shouts of revelers and assailants in the night as I went to bed.

I grew up in the Bronx. Not the South Bronx that famously burned while the Yankees played the Dodgers in game two of the 1977 World Series, but a working-class neighborhood in the Northwest Bronx called Norwood. We moved to the leafy, quiet, relatively affluent neighborhood of Riverdale when I was eleven, but then I began a daily commute into "the city," as we always called it, right as New York was setting crime records. The public magnet school I attended from seventh to twelfth grade was on the northernmost edge of the Upper East Side, adjacent to East Harlem. East Ninety-sixth Street made up the border. I knew every square foot and its potential danger. Or I should say, I thought I did. My biases and irrational neuroses colored everything about the physical experience of New York in the early 1990s. My own psychological makeup then was wired for anxiety, constantly hyperaware of my own self and its vulnerabilities as it moves through space. So for me, growing up in New York at the time of both peak violent crime and peak public panic about the same was a bit like taking a kid scared of roller coasters and raising him in an amusement park.

I don't think it's an overstatement to say that at some level, the thought of crime penetrated every single moment I spent walking the streets of New York. I'd scan the sidewalk for teenage boys who looked like they might be trouble. Often they were black or brown, but not always. There were many white hooligans to avoid as well. I'd cross the street. Then walk into a store, then another store. Then cross back and keep my head down. I'd avoid eye contact or, just at the moment where I sensed danger, ask an old lady for the time.

I learned a very particular gaze, eyes slightly downcast, so as not to make accidental eye contact and initiate hostility ("What the fuck you looking at?"), yet raised and open enough to constantly monitor possible threats in the periphery. I would tense myself for certain blocks. One friend lived on the Upper West Side on a block frequented by dealers (we opened the door to his house once to find a man passed out next to a crack pipe), and I'd need to work myself up into a lather of courage to stride purposefully down that block to his house. Particularly at night.

On the day in April 1992 when a Simi Valley jury found the police officers who beat Rodney King not guilty, the administrators of the school I attended panicked. They imagined that riots would break out in New York, so they let school out early and instructed students and teachers to go home and not linger on the streets. I was a thirteen-year-old eighth grader. A bunch of us went to the apartment of a friend who lived across the street. A little while after we got there, our friend's older brother came into the apartment with some upperclassmen, one of whom had just been punched in the face. The purple bruise around his eye seemed like a clear message: *This involves you too.*

I felt that threat personally and persistently, even though no one ever made it and even though I wasn't actually the target of much violence. I had a backpack jacked once. A few hats, I think. The only time I was actually attacked was on the night of a school dance. I was walking with a bunch of girls, the lone boy, feeling cocky, when a boy roughly my age came up to me and said, "Yo, can I see your bus pass." I hesitated. "I said, run your fuckin loot!" I had the thought in the moment to correct him: he hadn't actually said "Run your loot." But that thought was interrupted by him punching me in the chest and then knocking my wallet out of my hand as I withdrew it. He then whistled to a large group of friends, who appeared out of nowhere to ransack the contents. They took the few bucks in there and my bus pass (a city-issued pass for students that let them ride for free) and took off laughing.

Years later I can still conjure the shaking rage that consumed me, the burning humiliation and emasculation of being punched in the middle of the street for all to see. The city, seen through my teenage eyes, was spectacular but also ominous and exhausting.

I was bright enough to know that the same kids who jacked my backpack had had their own items jacked, and that they, too, lived in fear. But what was exceptional for me and my mostly white friends—violence—was far more likely to be routine in their world. That is: they were like me, scared teenagers full of bravado and terror in equal measure. But my actual feeling in that moment was that the space above the East Ninety-sixth Street border was an undifferentiated foreboding mass, a looming tower.

As I type this now, it all sounds ridiculous, overly dramatic. Was it really that bad? Well, at one level, yes. Those were the Crack Years, when crime, danger, and safety, consumed the city's politics and media. And not just because of irrational fear—the city really was more violent than it had been in many decades, perhaps ever. Lifelong New Yorkers of all races and ethnicities had never experienced anything like it. (Not that it was experienced "together" across racial lines in any meaningful sense.) In 1991, the year I started riding the bus down to Manhattan to attend a magnet school, New York City set a record with 2,245 homicides. In 2015, it had just 352. The year before I started junior high school, it had 100,280 robberies compared to 16,931 in 2015.

This was just one moment in a longer story. In a remarkably short period of time, America got much more dangerous for its citizens. In 1960 there were approximately 160 violent crimes for every 100,000 Americans. In a decade the violent crime rate more than doubled to 360, and by 1980 it reached nearly 600. The rate dipped briefly and then peaked in 1992 at around 750—an increase of more than 450 percent in less than four decades.

The brunt of the great American crime wave of the late 1960s and 1980s was borne not by frightened white people like myself but largely by poor people of color. In Washington, D.C., a majority-black city, drug-related homicides went up 500 percent in a single year, from 33 in 1988 to 154 in 1989. Ta-Nehisi Coates describes his own upbringing on the Westside of Baltimore during the Crack Years as drenched in fear.

> To be black in the Baltimore of my youth was to be
> naked before the elements of the world, before all

the guns, fists, knives, crack, rape, and disease. The
nakedness is not an error, nor pathology. The nakedness is the correct and intended result of policy, the
predictable upshot of people forced for centuries to
live under fear. The law did not protect us.

Fear of crime may have been preconditioned by centuries
of the American experience; it may have taken its particular
forms due to the pathologies embedded in America's racial
hierarchies. But that does not mean the fear was manufactured or invented as an excuse for what came after. Starting
in the 1960s, crime in America skyrocketed at an unprecedented pace. And not just the kinds of crimes that in later
years we would overpursue, the petty patrolling of traffic
violations and outstanding warrants and nonviolent drug
arrests. No: assaults, rapes, murders all went up.

And this violence created fear among citizens of all races,
as well as calls from deep within the Colony to do something
to stop it. This was certainly true in the Bronx of my youth. My
father Roger Hayes, a Jesuit-seminarian-turned-community-
organizer, co-founded the Northwest Bronx Community and
Clergy Coalition in 1974. These were the days when the Bronx
was burning, when the borough had become a global symbol of urban blight. The mission of the NWBCCC was to try
to prevent what had happened in the South Bronx—arson,
abandonment, violence, and devastation—from happening
to the Northwest Bronx. The group organized residents—
black, white, and Latino—to take on slumlords and orga-

nized tenants to demand services and repairs. It coordinated investment capital in places teetering on the brink of being reduced to rubble.

Key to the Alinsky-inspired method of community organizing that my dad and his colleagues practiced was that neighborhood residents set the priorities and made the demands. And as the Crack Years dawned in the late 1980s, community members became preoccupied with drugs and violence. Similar organizations around the country shifted their focus from redlining, affordable housing, and community investment to violence, crime, and drugs. "Organizing comes from what people are concerned about," my dad told me. "It wasn't that people weren't concerned about crime in the 1970s, but it really ramped up in the 1980s. And the crack thing was really huge. It was causing a lot of panic among people. People were seeing all of a sudden . . . all these people on the corner, all these people selling, all these people using. Whatever the low-level endemic drug issue was, it was ramped up a lot."

As James Forman, Jr., demonstrates in his excellent *Locking Up Our Own*, in the Crack Years black citizens, politicians, and activists understood drugs, crime, and violence as a near existential threat, one that rivaled the marauding destruction of earlier eras of white supremacist terrorism. "We have allowed death to change its name from Southern rope to Northern dope. Too many black youth have been victimized by pushing dope into their veins instead of hope into their brains," Jesse Jackson would say in 1991.

Forman cites example after example of prominent black political figures using some of the dehumanizing language that we've since come to associate with the racist overtones of law and order politics writ large. D.C. mayor Marion Barry railed against the "drug thugs and gun thugs," while Atlanta mayor Maynard Jackson said those sowing fear in his neighborhoods had to be "hunted down like dogs."

As crime hit historic highs, black people were terrified (in many neighborhoods for the most rational reasons), and white people were terrified (often completely out of proportion to the threat).

Because control over the machinery of the state in almost all places remained in the hands of an overwhelmingly white elite, a perverse form of "half-a-loaf" legislative compromise emerged during this period. Yes, black citizens, leaders, clergy, activists, and politicians in predominantly black neighborhoods recognized a crisis, and yes, they were demanding solutions. But the solutions they were demanding were full spectrum—more police *and* more jobs—while the solutions they got were entirely punitive.

In the fight over the 1994 crime bill, the NAACP excoriated the initial draft for its lack of investment in urban communities. The Congressional Black Caucus proposed its own alternative, with $5 billion more in funding for drug treatment and early intervention programs. But Republicans demagogued on the small amount of social spending in the Senate Democrats' version of the bill, railing against midnight basketball programs as a government subsidy for hooligans. The bill then lost an additional $2.5 billion in social spending, but left in place billions for prisons and a long list of punitive measures.

This process was repeated in statehouses and city halls across the country: black people asked for social investment and got SWAT teams, asked for full employment and got gang units, asked for protection and got "stop and frisk." White fear absorbed and appropriated black fear. Thanks to what scholars call "selective hearing," black fear, combined with white political power, produced a state committed to managing and punishing black and brown subjects rather than empowering and protecting them.

As Mariame Kaba, a prison abolition activist, wrote of arguments that African Americans were a significant constituency calling for getting tougher on crime and harsher punitive measures: "to say Black people wanted this too belies [the] fact that Blacks in the U.S. are AMERICANS. Americans LOVE punishment."

YEARS AGO, DURING A backpacking trip through South America, I was sitting in a café in a small town in Argentina, a few kilometers from one of the world's most beautiful waterfalls, marking the border with Brazil. My wife and I struck up a conversation with a fair-skinned man in his fifties. He was handsome and slightly aristocratic with a gray ponytail, and as he dramatically pulled drags off his cigarette, he spoke to the two young gringos in world-weary tones about the country just over the border "In Brazil," he said, "life is cheap. Especially among *los negros*."

What differentiates white fear as a social and political force from the fear felt by an individual—white or black, Latino or Asian, immigrant or native born—is the belief structure, often implicit and almost never articulated, in which that fear rests. If life across the border is cheap, if violence is routine and tragedy a habit, then, the logic goes, "they" don't experience fear the same way. On the other hand, "we"—the collective social we, we the people who have relative privilege, the hardworking (white) folks, who have come so far, who are so upstanding and special, should not have to fear. Sure in the ghettos, it's scary, but for *them* fear is just part of life. It's easier for them.

In 2015, a few days after the unrest in Baltimore, I stood outside city hall with three young men from the Westside. They grew up in Freddie Gray's neighborhood, and two lived there still. The third man, the oldest of the group, had managed, after a stint in prison, to move out to the suburbs. They'd spent the day delivering groceries and goods to seniors in a housing development in the neighborhood at the heart of the unrest. They chuckled as they watched my TV live shot, and we struck up a conversation. Over the next forty minutes they reeled off a list of acts of violence and crime that they had witnessed or been victims of. The tally seemed incomprehensible. The youngest of them had had his sister taken from him when she was fourteen in a brutal murder on the Baltimore public transit. The other two had lost best friends, cousins, and uncles. And then the oldest man described the sheer ecstatic relief of his new life in the suburbs. "I can breathe," I remember him saying. "Just sit outside and breathe."

Later that year, after homicides spiked by 63 percent in Baltimore in 2015, a barber told my producer that twenty people whose hair had been cut in his shop had been murdered. Discussions of death had become "like saying, you know, 'I brushed my teeth this morning,'" because the onslaught had become so routine. "That's all we talk about."

Opponents of Black Lives Matter protesters often make a strange, disingenuous pivot. They cite the devastation that violent crime wreaks among black Americans as a rebuttal to the claim that police are killing black people. But violent deaths at the hands of the police and those at the hands of gang members don't exist in some kind of competition. They are two sides of the same coin. When those outside the Colony point with derision at the violence within it to justify its continued existence, they reinforce how undervalued black lives are.

In ways large and small and constant, the Nation exhibits contempt for the lives of its subjects in the Colony and indifference to their value. This is the central component of the white fear that sustains the Colony: the simple inability to recognize, deeply, fully totally, the humanity of those on the other side. It's why the wave of protests has come to so many white people as such a surprise. The systematic devaluation of the Colony is so remarkably well hidden, so easily unseen.

"When we are waiting for our clients to arrive from the county jail in the morning, the deputies, the district attorneys, and the judges refer to our clients as 'bodies,'" Oakland public defender Seth Morris once told me. "'Are the bodies here yet? We have files but no bodies.' I once asked a deputy to call my client a human being, and I was laughed at."

One way the state expresses value for life is in its pursuit of those who take it. Homicide is the gravest crime of all. Violations of laws against extinguishing another person's life should be most vigorously investigated and punished. And yet the national clearance rate for homicides was only 64 percent in 2012. The rate varies by locality, however, and in many large American cities—where the overwhelming majority of murder victims are black and brown—the clearance rates are even below 50 percent. Ferguson reported clearing 100 percent of murder and nonnegligent manslaughter cases in 2012 and 2013. New York City cleared around 72 percent of cases in 2013 and 2014. Baltimore, though, averaged a clearance rate of 47 percent for 2011 to 2014.

Perhaps most remarkably, over the past several decades, as crime has declined at historically unprecedented rates, as more cops have been hired and more resources have been poured into policing, that clearance rate has actually gone down in many places. Back in 1965 the national clearance rate was 90 percent. Even as homicides decline and the number of cops rises, police are getting worse at catching murderers.

Jill Leovy, who chronicled the work of homicide detectives in South Central Los Angeles in her masterful book *Ghettoside*, argues that this inability to solve and punish the most serious crimes is the flip side of a system that overpunishes minor infractions. "Like the schoolyard bully, our criminal justice system harasses people on small pretexts but is exposed as a coward before murder. It hauls masses of black men through its machinery but fails to protect them from bodily injury and death. It is at once oppressive and inadequate."

When it comes to the ultimate punishment, death, the system makes clear which lives it values: the best predictor of whether someone gets the death penalty is race—not of the perpetrator but of the victim. White lives are far more likely to merit, in the eyes of courts, juries, and prosecutors, the ultimate punishment. White lives matter, and it hardly needs to be spoken.

The disparate value of life is painfully clear to people living in the Colony. Cynthia Swann, fifty-five, a resident of Southwest Baltimore, came out to survey the aftermath of the Freddie Gray unrest the day after the CVS burned. She told me she "became civically active when the police killed another police officer and no one was indicted." In January 2011, she recounted, William Torbit, a black Baltimore cop, had been in plainclothes outside a nightclub in the middle of a fight. Several Baltimore police officers were called to respond to the melee, and when they arrived, they shot and killed him (as well as a twenty-two-year-old civilian). "There was never any indictment. Nothing was ever done about it," Swann told me.

She compared Torbit's case to that of Baltimore police officer Jeffrey Bolger, who in June 2014 responded to a call where a dog had bitten someone. When he arrived, he slit the dog's throat. The officer, Swann pointed out, was immediately suspended and ultimately prosecuted. (He would later be acquitted). There was a lesson here about how much the system valued black life. The contrast between these two cases, she said, "tells the community and the children that an animal's life is worth more than your life."

This is why "Black Lives Matter" has emerged as such a simple, powerful rebuke to the unstated premise of the Colony's existence. It simply asserts a basic principle that should need no enunciation. Yet the phrase has inspired intense backlash. Opponents have attempted to twist its meaning into "*Only* Black Lives Matter." But save for a few kooky Black Israelites who used to rant black supremacist sermons in Times Square during my youth, it's safe to say that no one believes "only black lives matter." No, "Black Lives Matter" means "Black Lives Matter, Too."

The backlash is rooted in the way white fear operates. In the days after the Freddie Gray unrest, quite a few Baltimore residents—all white—wanted to tell me the "real story" of Freddie Gray. Like right-wing e-mail forwards, they often attributed the "real story" to a "friend who's a cop" who was in a position to know the truth—as opposed to the "politically correct" cover story being spun by District Attorney Marilyn Mosby. I heard numerous times that Gray had actually run from the cops because he was carrying drugs (he was a dealer, all these people took pains to point out), then had jumped out the window of one of the projects in Sandtown Winchester. The fall had been what snapped his spine. "They don't want to let that get out," one man told me, puffing a cigarette while warily watching the protesters outside city hall, "because now it's all politics."

These rumors were all nonsense—definitively false, as established by the medical examiner. But they were almost desperate attempts to will away the obvious fact that Gray's death was an injustice. The idea that he was an innocent victim did not compute. Even in death he was presumed guilty, because he had been a denizen of the Colony, and c'mon, everyone there is guilty of something. Or in the infamous words used to describe Michael Brown, "he was no angel." In the popular imagination, the Colony is a land that doesn't breed angels.

To deny Freddie Gray his innocence is part of the machinery of repression that makes white fear so potent. Along with causing the Nation to undervalue the lives of those in the Colony, white fear also expresses the forbidden knowledge that all white people carry with them: *We've got it better.* And if white people have it better, then isn't it only logical that black people will try to come and take what they have?

"They were coming downtown from a world of crack, welfare, guns, knives, indifference and ignorance," famed New
York newspaper columnist Pete Hamill wrote of the group of
young black men who had allegedly gang-raped and beaten
a white woman jogging in Central Park in 1989.

> They were coming from a land with no fathers. . . .
> They were coming from the anarchic province of
> the poor. And driven by a collective fury, brimming
> with the rippling energies of youth, their minds
> teeming with the violent images of the streets and
> the movies, they had only one goal: to smash, hurt,
> rob, stomp, rape. The enemies were rich. The ene-
> mies were white.

Of course, the "they" in Hamill's column turned out to be
innocent. The story of marauding black and Latino teens in
the white precincts of Central Park raping and pillaging was
nothing more than a dark urban fairy tale (though that was
only definitively established after five innocent young men
had done a collective fifty years in prison).

Hamill's column was by no means an outlier. In fact, for
a long stretch of my late childhood and adolescence, such
rhetoric was more or less the default register of the New York
media. "They"—the black and brown subjects of the Colony,
the denizens of the "anarchic province of the poor"—are
angry and wild and uncivilized and are coming for us, to
take what "we" have.

White fear emanates from knowing that white privilege exists and the anxiety that it might end. No matter how many white people tell pollsters that "today discrimination against whites has become as big a problem as discrimination against blacks" (60 percent of the white working class in one poll), we know that this story of antiwhite bias is not true. But we do know that having it "better" isn't permanent, that it could collapse. We know equality might someday come, and it might mean giving up one's birthright or, more terrifyingly, having it taken away. That perhaps our destiny is indeed a more equal society, but one where equality means equal misery, a social order where all the plagues of the "ghetto" escape past its borders and infect the population at large.

PETE HAMILL WASN'T FEAR-MONGERING on his own—he was involved in something bigger than himself. White fear is a collaborative production. A crowd can act in wild, terrifying, ecstatic ways, far beyond the cruelty of a single individual. Similarly, white fear is a collective experience: it is greater than the sum of its parts. It is neither a pure, organic, grassroots expression of the people, nor simply a construction of demagogues and elite guardians of white racial hierarchy. It is cultivated through a kind of call-and-response between speaker and crowd, between politicians and voters, between media and audience.

I understand this process far, far better now than I ever

have. For several years I have worked in an industry that frankly thrives on fear. The job of TV news is to grab the attention of the viewer, and the most effective way to do so is to reach out through the screen, past the frontal cortex of the brain, the area of higher reasoning and consciousness, and straight down into the brainstem, where the most ancient, animalistic survival instincts hum and pulse. We are wired to identify threats, not to process statistics. And when it's your job to grab attention, you learn to trigger those threat neurons over and over. We mash the keys until they're worn out.

So, to take just one example: during the great Ebola panic of 2014, only one person died in the United States, but a poll in November of that year found Americans identifying it as a more urgent priority than any other disease, "including cancer or heart disease, which together account for nearly half of all U.S. deaths each year." In fact, in a typical year more Americans are literally killed by their own furniture than are killed by terrorists, but when you ask them, they will tell you they are far more scared of terrorism than of nearly any other threat.

In fact, if you look at the American obsession with crime and then terrorism, you see a kind of crossfade between the two: in the aftermath of 9/11, as the War on Terror ramped up, the American obsession with crime began to wane.

Recent history can account for this shift. Law and order and the War on Drugs were a reaction to the real and genuinely scary escalation of crime, a reaction that dissipated as crime came down. Then the War on Terror was a reaction to a horrifying, unprecedented event: the 9/11 attacks and subsequent attacks by Al Qaeda and other jihadist groups such as ISIS. This story is on its face true.

But it's also easy to see, in the smooth segue between these fixations, the churning neuroses of white fear seeking their expression, looking for the next threat to guard against and subdue. Sometimes the threats are on the frontier, sometimes in the fieldhouse, sometimes in the adjacent neighborhood, and sometimes in the dark men plotting halfway around the world. Certain people outside our borders—literal or metaphorical—wish to do us harm, and they must be brought to heel. George H. W. Bush beat the Massachusetts liberal Michael Dukakis by deploying terrifying images of Willie Horton; his son beat another Massachusetts liberal with images of the Twin Towers falling.

The wolf is always at the door. It just changes its clothing.

In fact, the War on Terror has, in so many ways, played out like the law and order obsession with crime that preceded it. Events grounded in truth—the crime rate really was rising in an unprecedented fashion, and the worst attack in the history of the Republic really did take place—morphed into panic. The panic then became so widespread that the communal experience of it—the urgent white fear that citizens, politicians, and media all collaborated in producing—overrode the reality that it was reacting to. Mass incarceration almost certainly wouldn't have happened had crime not spiked the way it did. But mass incarceration was by no means the only available response to that spike. The War on Terror wouldn't have happened without 9/11, and any society attacked like that would have responded, but 9/11 didn't mean that an open-ended, multitrillion-dollar global war was the natural or appropriate response.

Through our shared cultural inheritance, Americans convert white fear into policy. When the system receives a shock—a crime wave, a terrorist attack—and we must answer the question *What is to be done*, our collective response is punishment, toughness, and violence. We build a bureaucracy and vocabulary of toughness that then take on their own power, their own gravity and inertia. We then bequeath the institutions of toughness to the next generation of politicians and policy makers, even after the initial problem they were meant to solve has dissipated.

Because white fear is a constant, because it persists even when specific threats have subsided, it functions as a one-way ratchet in constructing the architecture of the Colony. It can build prisons but not knock them down. For decades, Gallup has been asking Americans if they think crime has gone up, gone down, or stayed roughly the same. Every year since 2002 a majority of Americans have told Gallup crime had gone up the previous year, even though, in all but one year, it had declined. In fact, between 1993 and 2014 the rate of crime victimization fell from about 80 to 20 per 1,000, but by the end of that period, a full 63 percent of respondents still told Gallup crime had "gone up" in the previous year.

In 2016 Gallup found American's fears of crime hit a fifteen-year high, even as crime itself was near historic lows.

Undoubtedly the atmosphere around crime and policing today is worlds different from what it was in, say, 1968 or 1989 or 1994. Incarceration in many states is actually declining, and the beginnings of something like a political consensus—however tenuous and uneasy—has formed, between left and right, that locking up millions of our own citizens has been an expensive, tragic, and embarrassing mistake.

But the law and order demagoguery of Donald Trump's presidential campaign, its aggressive celebration of white fear—of terrorists, immigrants, and black criminals—shows just how weak that consensus is.

Because white fear is always waiting in the wings. In Ferguson, the fear felt by the nonprotesting, overwhelmingly white citizens of the Nation was palpable. The people I met putting up "I Heart Ferguson" signs in a local coffee shop spoke with pride about the quiet orderliness and the trustworthiness of the police. But there were problems, of course, they would say vaguely, leaving you to fill in the blanks.

Problem areas.

Problem blocks.

Problem people.

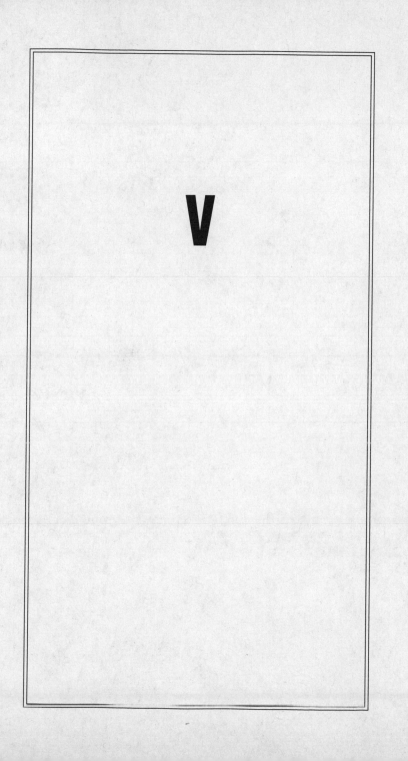

V

The New York of my childhood was *seedy*. It's a word my parents used a lot, though I almost never hear it these days. That may be because the condition it named has been so thoroughly, triumphantly banished; or perhaps *sketchy* has replaced it. Seediness was everywhere in the New York of the 1980s and '90s, in the streets and subways and neighborhoods as well as in representations of the city in TV and film.

In its most common usage, seediness has to do with vice. A red-light district is seedy; it's a place where no one wants their face seen. But in the context of New York, the adjective had descriptive force far beyond the peep shows on Eighth Avenue in midtown. (I remember clearly driving past them in the car with my family on the way home from visiting my aunt in Greenwich Village. We fell awkwardly silent in the presence of so much concentrated and unabashed seediness.)

Seediness was distinct from, but still somehow related to, danger. A neighborhood could be seedy but not necessarily dangerous. The iconically seedy Times Square of the 1990s never had particularly high violent crime rates, at least nowhere near as high as in the city's poorest neighborhoods, where gun violence was commonplace. But if Washington Heights and East New York and the South Bronx came to represent New York at its most dangerous, Times Square was New York at its seediest. Denizens of porn shops, peep shows, and SROs, vagabonds, homeless men and women, people struggling with addiction or mental health crises, panhandlers, hustlers—all congregated on the streets. People who lived on the edges of society took up physical space in the public square at the very center of the physical city.

Of course, the phenomenon of urban illicitness is by no means limited to New York. Parts of every major city in America had the same problems, from Boston to San Francisco to Washington, D.C., where drug deals happened in Lafayette Park just across from the North Lawn of the White House. In these venues, the political problems that seediness caused and the policy solutions it demanded had nothing to do with the actual people and populations who were causing it: people in need of clothing, housing, drug treatment, and mental health services. They themselves were the problem, and the solution was to do something with them rather than do anything for them.

Even to this day, the discussion around homelessness in major cities, New York included, focuses primarily on the problem of nonhomeless people *seeing too many homeless people,* not on the problem of too many people lacking homes. This was a core problem of seediness for New York's powers that be: who wanted to open a business with riffraff squatting outside, scaring customers at all hours of the day and night?

More than anything, seediness imposed a kind of mental tax on certain strata of the middle to upper classes, the mostly white city dwellers and commuters who found the ambient unruliness stressful. The sense of menace and chaos that hung about made residents and tourists alike uncomfortable.

The somewhat infamous "squeegee men" epitomized that unease, which I remember feeling myself when my family would drive around Manhattan to visit my mom's sisters. At a red light, a squeegee man (almost always black) would approach the car and begin washing the windshield with a squeegee. When he'd finished, you'd give him some change or a buck or two.

Something about the exchange was slightly intimidating. He didn't ask you if you wanted your window cleaned; he just started doing it, with the expectation that once he was finished, you the driver would compensate him for his labor. And this forced the driver to make a decision: either he would hold fast to his initial desire not to pay for a pointless window cleaning, and perhaps face the wrath of the man who'd just done it, or he would allow himself to be manipulated into paying the man for a service he'd never wanted and never requested.

I'll stress again that this phenomenon was quite distinct from the massive spike in crime. These interactions might've been unpleasant and uncomfortable and maybe, under the strictest reading of New York statutes, illegal, but they were in no way violent. They were an incursion. They were the city reaching into your car and forcing you to reckon with it.

Urban seediness was the opposite of suburban tranquility. In fact, the suburbs were where you fled to escape seediness, to protect your children from it. The suburbs were clean, and the city was dirty. The suburbs enjoyed empty streets, while city streets hosted vagabonds and drug addicts. More than anything else, the suburbs were *orderly*—with houses, lawns, people, and cars all in their place. The city was disorderly, a tangle of people and noise and unclear rules.

Seediness in this specific urban context wasn't reducible solely to race—the gutter punks hanging out in seedy Tompkins Square Park or loitering on St. Marks Place in the Village were mostly white—but it was inextricably connected to it. During much of the twentieth century, the great migration of black people out of the South had made America's cities, from New York to Chicago to Detroit to L.A., places of concentrated blackness. And even as the de jure segregation in the Jim Crow South was being slowly dismantled, the long-standing de facto segregation of housing and schooling in the North intensified. Federal policy facilitated both the construction of the "ghetto," large areas of black residents and disinvestment, and white flight to the suburbs, abetted by subsidized mortgages and racially discriminatory lending guidelines.

By the mid-1960s, cities outside the Deep South had become front lines of American racial struggle. Watts erupted in flames, and Martin Luther King, Jr., marched through Chicago, greeted by white people shouting "Niggers go home!" and chucking bottles. He encountered such venom, he said that white people in Chicago could teach white people in Mississippi "how to hate."

AT THE MICRO LEVEL, the Nation's anxiety over racial equality and coexistence manifested as concerns about "the neighborhood," as in "there it goes." In the years when black people were moving into neighborhoods in, say, the formerly white ethnic enclaves of the Bronx, crime was also going up. These events were unrelated, but they were easily and at times eagerly conflated by white residents, politicians, and predatory realtors. A semantic shift occurred. Now one could talk about race without ever mentioning the word *black*. The legendary Republican political operative Lee Atwater once described the way this worked at the national level.

> You start out in 1954 by saying, "Nigger, nigger, nigger." By 1968 you can't say "nigger"—that hurts you. Backfires. So you say stuff like forced busing, states' rights and all that stuff. You're getting so abstract now [that] you're talking about cutting taxes, and all these things you're talking about are totally eco-

nomic things and a byproduct of them is [that] blacks
get hurt worse than whites.

In the context of urban politics, it worked somewhat differently. The key sites of battle weren't tax cuts and budgets.
Instead, residents and politicians could speak of property
values or crime, and then even further removed, they could
say the concern was litter or graffiti or abandoned buildings.
They weren't lying: they were, at some level, actually concerned with the creeping seediness of the city. But American racial history—the nation's most enduring and violently
loaded conflict—lurked even in the municipal disputes of
my youth, as the virus of racism infected neighborhood politics and bloomed in tabloid headlines.

Of course, a lot of the time racial conflict wasn't subtext. In
1986 four black men walked into the white Queens neighborhood of Howard Beach after their car broke down. They were
chased and beaten by a white mob. As twenty-three-year-old
Michael Griffith, one of the four, attempted to evade the mob,
he was struck by a car and died. Just three years later four
black teenagers went to the white ethnic Brooklyn neighborhood of Bensonhurst to inquire about a used Pontiac for sale.
They were met by a mob of white men wielding baseball bats,
and one, a man named Joseph Fama, was carrying a gun. The
mob beat the young black men, and then Fama fired two shots
into the chest of sixteen-year-old Yusef Hawkins, killing him.

The mob had apparently been lying in wait for another
group of black and Latino men who they believed were com-

ing to the neighborhood. It was a lynching, plain and simple, more than six decades after the Dyer anti-lynching bill was introduced (and never passed), and over two hundred miles north of the Mason-Dixon line.

This level of virulent white racism wasn't limited to a few isolated neighborhoods—it could be found throughout the city. In fact, I spent much of my childhood in one of those places. The Italian American neighborhood Morris Park in the Bronx, where I went to elementary school, featured delicious pizza, single-family homes, and tidy yards with fig trees wrapped in blankets and trash bags to keep them warm in the winter. It was also, in the mid-1980s, the kind of place where certain adults would drop the word *nigger* casually.

Not by accident, one of the chief architects of Nixon's highly effective racialized Southern Strategy, which led white southerners away from the Democratic Party and into the arms of Nixon, Reagan, and the Republicans, was the definitively nonsouthern Kevin Phillips, a white Bronx native of the Parkchester neighborhood, adjacent to Morris Park. His first political job was staffing a Republican congressman from the Bronx who ran the borough's Republican party and represented Morris Park among other ethnic enclaves.

In 1970 Phillips was contemptuous of attempts by liberal Republicans to persuade black voters to join the party, telling a *Times* reporter:

> From now on the Republicans are never going to get more than 10 to 20 per cent of the Negro vote and

they don't need any more than that . . . but Republicans would be shortsighted if they weakened enforcement of the Voting Rights Act. The more Negroes
who register as Democrats in the South, the sooner
the Negrophobe whites will quit the Democrats and
become Republicans. That's where the votes are.

This wasn't a Mississippian but a New Yorker talking about
the benefits of backlash politics and the advantages of bringing "negrophobes" into the Republican Party. As the *Times*
profile noted, Phillips

had grown up in the Bronx. His observations of life
in this polyglot borough had convinced him that all
the talk about melting pot America was buncombe.
Most voters, he had found, still voted on the basis of
ethnic or cultural enmities that could be graphed,
predicted and exploited.

The kind of raw and bitter New York racial battles that
formed Phillips's worldview, and that swirled everywhere
around me in the city of my youth, now largely take place
through the lens of gentrification, an inversion of the old
"there goes the neighborhood" politics of white flight.

But today in inner-ring suburbs around the country, worry
that the neighborhood is going to seed is a constant preoc-
cupation. In many metropolitan regions, urban real estate
price spikes have pushed the poor out into the periphery.

Areas that were once squarely in the Nation now see the Colony flooding over the border. In these places, the freighted municipal battles of the Bronx of my youth are reinscribing themselves. North Charleston, South Carolina, a once-white suburb, is now majority black—and a black man fleeing a traffic stop was shot in the back by a white police officer. Ferguson, Missouri—like many parts of the Bronx—went from majority white to majority black in a relatively short period of time. "A lot of people have left here," Ferguson's white mayor, James Knowles, told me. By which he meant, I think, *A lot of white people have left here.* He continued, "There is also a lot of people that have stayed here and enjoyed that diversity."

After a few days of talking to Ferguson residents, I recognized a familiar dynamic: the cheek-by-jowl racial politics of a large metropolis was now churning through a town of 20,000 residents. As in New York in the 1980s, Ferguson's racial composition had changed, but its governing class hadn't kept up. Ferguson's white residents spoke a lot about the parts of the town that were unruly, unkempt—seedy—notably the Section 8 rental apartments on Canfield Drive where Mike Brown was shot and killed, a one-block stretch of the Colony.

"You know, Canfield Apartments [are] one of the things we have struggled with for the past few years," the mayor told me. "There is a lot of subsidized housing over there, a lot of people do not stay very long. A lot of people they come and go." *Disorderly,* in other words.

I asked him what he thought was the big takeaway from the death of Michael Brown and the protests for racial justice that had brought hundreds of reporters from around the world to his city.

The mayor didn't hesitate: "We have to find a way to stabilize housing. There is, all across north St. Louis County, a problem with housing where people only live for a few years. They switch school districts, you know, every year. They move houses every year, every six months. They never really set down roots. We have to find a way to do that."

I was a bit incredulous: "So you think that is sort of the— that is your takeaway from this?

"Yeah, the takeaway is we have to find a way to stabilize them here in the community and make them part of it."

Ah yes, *stabilize housing*—that phrase was familiar to me, like concerns about vagrants and seediness and orderliness. Stability is one of the things that, in the minds of those within the Nation, define it, compared to the transience of the Colony. I'm sure the mayor really was concerned with making sure his constituents had a stake in the city and felt part of it for the long term. But the subtext was present, too: that it was the denizens of the Colony who were causing problems, and things would be fine if Ferguson could get rid of this disorderly class of squatters who had infiltrated their town.

In the Bronx of my youth, the specter of danger, disorder, and seediness manifested physically in abandoned and burned-out buildings. I found the mayor's statement about stability slightly amusing because Canfield Apartments—a small cluster of tidy low-rise buildings featuring a communal yard and balconies on a tree-lined block—would have seemed thoroughly suburban even in Morris Park, and much more so in the South Bronx districts of Morrisania or Hunts Point.

Popular representations of the Bronx during the 1980s portrayed it as a literal war zone: rubble, decay, destruction, and abandonment. The footage of Ronald Reagan visiting the South Bronx on a hot summer day in 1980 looks like a head of state's visit to a hostile country overseas. Black and brown bodies surround his white staff and detail, and in the background looms the uncanny landscape of an urban neighborhood so bereft of buildings you can see the actual horizon in the shot.

In a hilarious attempt to slap a Band-Aid on urban blight, the administration of Mayor Ed Koch covered the windows of dozens of city-owned abandoned buildings with full-length decals of venetian blinds or a shade partially drawn over a colorful flower box, as if to say *Look someone lives here and cares for this window! This is not an abandoned building in a crushingly destitute warren of the Colony left to rot by the powers that be!*

Of course, no one apparently could be troubled to vary the window decals much. (Let's not get too crazy with our Potemkin makeover of one of the poorest places in the city.) Driving through the Bronx in the 1990s, you would look up to see rows of identical window box decals staring down from an obviously abandoned building. I remember having childlike daydreams about who put them there, and what it would be like to have the job of window-stickerer, spending one's working hours in spooky, empty structures. The cumulative effect was precisely the opposite of its intent; the orderly rows of identical sunny stickers affixed to the hollow skeleton of a building that once housed urban life looked chilling and dystopian.

The intended audience for these stickers, of course, wasn't the residents of the Bronx. They were mostly applied in city-owned abandoned buildings that faced major thoroughfares like the Cross Bronx Expressway, which thousands of non-Bronx residents passed during their daily commute. Residents of the borough were largely unenthused. One resident told a *New York Times* reporter "They should fix up the buildings, and have people living here, not decals."

"Somebody doesn't care," said another, "or they'd be making homes for people rather than making missiles and giving us decals." All the while, Mayor Koch defended the much-mocked stickers. "In a neighborhood, as in life, a clean bandage is much, much better than a raw or festering wound."

"Festering wounds" were everywhere to be found in the city at that point. New York was an empire in disrepair. It was unruly. Above all else, from the street crime to the graffiti to the boom boxes, it was *disorderly*. The city was in physical decline. The subways were covered with graffiti, streets were strewn with trash, and across all five boroughs one could see thousands and thousands of broken windows.

BROKEN WINDOWS: A SIMPLE, casual fact of urban blight. These two words would become one of the most powerful phrases in the history of American criminology.

Given the folklore around "broken windows" as the silver bullet that once and for all slayed the urban crime monster, it's a trip to go back and actually read the article that started it all. Published in 1982 in the *Atlantic*, "Broken Windows: The Police and Neighborhood Safety" opens with a gloss of a report from the Police Foundation in Washington on the results of a New Jersey state experiment in which officers were pushed out of their cars onto foot patrols.

The controlled experiment did *not* produce a reduction in the actual crime rate, and yet according to the authors, George L. Kelling and James Q. Wilson, "residents of the foot patrolled neighborhoods seemed to feel more secure than persons in other areas, tended to believe that crime had been reduced, and seemed to take fewer steps to protect themselves from crime (staying at home with the doors locked, for example)."

Though the theory would later be simplified to suggest that one could reduce crime by stamping out disorder—drunkenness, public urination, sidewalk gambling—the authors were actually making a far more modest claim. They were interested in psychology. Police, they argued, could be used to make people feel safer even if they weren't actually improving overall safety:

> Many citizens, of course, are primarily frightened by crime, especially crime involving a sudden, violent

attack by a stranger. This risk is very real, in Newark as in many large cities. But we tend to overlook
another source of fear—the fear of being bothered
by disorderly people. Not violent people, nor, necessarily, criminals, but disreputable or obstreperous or
unpredictable people: panhandlers, drunks, addicts,
rowdy teenagers, prostitutes, loiterers, the mentally
disturbed. What foot-patrol officers did was to ele-
vate, to the extent they could, the level of public order
in these neighborhoods. Though the neighborhoods
were predominantly black and the foot patrolmen
were mostly white, this "order-maintenance" function of the police was performed to the general satis-
faction of both parties.

Kelling and Wilson were explicitly offering a police strategy designed to produce a collective psychological effect, one
intended to satiate the neuroses of anxious urban dwellers
who worried that the neighborhood was going downhill, and
to stem the contagion that came with that unraveling. "A sta-
ble neighborhood of families who care for their homes, mind
each other's children, and confidently frown on unwanted
intruders can change," they observed, "in a few years or even
a few months, to an inhospitable and frightening jungle."

The jungle. The primordial land of disorder and unruly
natives, the precincts outside civilization's control. And this
disorder, they suggested, could also eventually lead to crime
in a self-fulfilling vicious circle.

At the community level, disorder and crime are usually inextricably linked, in a kind of developmental
sequence. Social psychologists and police officers
tend to agree that if a window in a building is broken
and is left unrepaired, all the rest of the windows
will soon be broken. This is as true in nice neighborhoods as in rundown ones. Window-breaking does
not necessarily occur on a large scale because some
areas are inhabited by determined window-breakers
whereas others are populated by window-lovers;
rather, one unrepaired broken window is a signal
that no one cares, and so breaking more windows
costs nothing. (It has always been fun.)

Kelling spent time with a white Newark foot patrolman
he called Kelly and watched as he enforced order in a rundown but bustling transit hub in the city: telling teenagers
to quiet down, instructing drunks to keep their bottles in
paper bags and drink only on side streets rather than the
major thoroughfares: "Sometimes what Kelly did could be
described as 'enforcing the law,'" Kelling and Wilson noted,
"but just as often it involved taking informal or extralegal
steps to help protect what the neighborhood had decided
was the appropriate level of public order. Some of the things
he did probably would not withstand a legal challenge."

Here we see one of the earliest articulations of the the-
oretical distinction between the Colony and the Nation.
Newark circa 1982 was a city in the midst of massive white

flight in the wake of pitched battles over school busing and housing integration. It was poor and mostly black. Kelling and Wilson were arguing, unapologetically, that in these precincts of the Colony, order should matter more than law.

Hundreds of years of historical weight rode on such a pronouncement, and yet the authors repeatedly referenced race only to quickly wave it away. At a few moments they seemed painfully unaware of their own racial blind spots. "Our experience," they wrote, "is that most citizens like to talk to a police officer."

Really?

"Broken windows" was an impulse before it was a theory. Kelling and Wilson were up front about the fact they were offering nothing new but rather a return to the "folk wisdom" of those residents who believed that disorder was contagious. They fondly recalled the good old days, when cops could just do whatever they felt necessary to keep the toughs in line.

> The police in this earlier period assisted in that reas-
> sertion of authority by acting, sometimes violently, on
> behalf of the community. Young toughs were roughed
> up, people were arrested "on suspicion" or for vagrancy,
> and prostitutes and petty thieves were routed. "Rights"
> were something enjoyed by decent folk.

This last line about rights is important. Kelling and Wilson seem implicitly to have been hostile to the kind of rights-based proceduralism that flowed from the Warren Court.

They were urging the return to a bygone era when cops were local authorities who enforced community norms of order, rather than enforcers of the law within the confines of explicit constitutional rights. They suggested that police could help a community maintain order, but that the standards for order must come from the community itself.

In this sense, the "broken windows" approach began as a call for what liberals today approvingly call "community policing"—the "community" and the police collaborating to identify problems and protect citizens. The article is predicated on a study that required cops to get out of their cars and actually walk their beats, a key pillar of today's "community policing." Yet in the modern vocabulary of policing theory, "broken windows" has become shorthand for the polar opposite: aggressive, community-antagonistic, clean-'em-up vigilantism.

The problem with "community policing," then and now, is that so often the cops being called to enforce community norms are not part of the community. And Kelling and Wilson's celebrated "earlier period" of lone wolf policing looks pretty different to black residents of major cities. In the study that inspired the article, the cops were almost all white and the citizens of the Newark neighborhoods almost all black. Just how likely was it that hundreds of young white men in inner-city Newark were going to be the vessels through which that predominantly African American community enforced its own norms and order? Kelling and Wilson recognized this problem but ultimately shrugged their shoulders.

How do we ensure that age or skin color or national origin or harmless mannerisms will not also become the basis for distinguishing the undesirable from the desirable? How do we ensure, in short, that the police do not become the agents of neighborhood bigotry?

We can offer no wholly satisfactory answer to this important question.

And yet Kelling and Wilson offered a comforting vision, at least for some: police as neighborhood watchmen, telling the unruly boys to knock it off and helping the old ladies cross the street. Assessing the city after desegregation and the great crime wave, they gave expression to and quasi-social-scientific justification for a generalized feeling, a hunch, lying in the white American subconscious: that all this disorder, this dirtiness, this filth and graffiti and brokenness must be cleaned. It must be washed. It must be ordered. This was the cri de coeur of the (oddly sympathetic) sociopathic Travis Bickle, who surveyed the New York of 1976 in *Taxi Driver* and said,

All the animals come out at night.

Whores, skunk pussies, buggers, queens, fairies, dopers, junkies.

Sick, venal.

Someday a real rain will come and wash this scum off the streets.

As a theory, "broken windows" played a perfect explanatory role for politicians and policy makers. If disorder leads to crime, well then, we need to crack down on disorder. And cracking down on disorder was something the police could do. The liberal theory of the causes of crime—that it was born of racism, segregation, oppression, poverty, and disinvestment—painted a picture of the problem that required a set of solutions far above what the local beat cops could provide. The federal and state governments would have to not just cooperate with such an agenda but prioritize it, mobilize for the domestic policy equivalent of war. Wealth would have to be redistributed, students would have to be bused, housing laws would have to be enforced, and on and on. Getting rid of the "ghetto" as an institution would require a full, multigenerational commitment to making racial equality a genuine, lived economic reality in America. That was a social project for which, frankly, white voters had (and continue to have) little appetite.

"Broken windows," on the other hand, offered an elegantly simple and eminently implementable program. No need for messy discussions about integration, equality, racial justice, and capital flows. No need to face the wrath of angry parents at town halls furious that their kids were being sent to a "bad school" thirty minutes away. Just start enforcing order, and the signal would be sent to criminals to behave.

Back in 1982, when Kelling and Wilson wrote their famous article, they didn't even pretend to claim that enforcing order would lead to reductions in crime. Their argument was about the sentiment of the community (making residents "feel" safer). And they threw up their hands at the intractability of crime in the most desolately disinvested neighborhoods: "Some neighborhoods are so demoralized and crime-ridden as to make foot patrol useless."

Despite these caveats, "broken windows" soon became an article of faith among the nation's law enforcement leaders, chief among them Bill Bratton, who had been hired in 1990 to run the police department of New York's transit authority. Kelling had been hired in 1985 as a consultant. Bratton embraced the man as his intellectual mentor and set about putting his theory into practice, ramping up enforcement of fare jumping, graffiti, and open containers. The highly publicized results were striking to even casual commuters: the subways became cleaner, less graffiti-riddled, and more pleasant to occupy. The year after Bratton assumed office, the total number of violent crimes in the subways declined 15 percent.

Three years later, when Rudy Giuliani was elected on a "quality of life" platform that promised, in its own way, to wash the city clean with a "real rain," Bratton was promoted to take over the entire NYPD. He set about ridding the city of the scourge of the squeegee men, who for Giuliani had become a kind of iconic symbol of the city's disorder.

At this very moment crime in America reached a national tipping point. In 1993 crime started dropping in pretty much all categories nationwide, and then it just kept dropping. Nowhere in the country did it drop as swiftly or as dramatically as New York City. "While there is some variance by type of crime, the best rule of thumb for comparing the magnitude of New York City's crime decline to that of the rest of the United States is that any crime drop for the rest of the United States is doubled in New York City," criminologist Franklin Zimring observes. "In the same spirit that media were prone to choose a city as the 'murder capital' of the United States when crime statistics were issued, New York City was beyond dispute the Crime Decline Capital of the United States in the 1990s."

Bratton became the face of this crime decline, featured on the cover of *Time* magazine in 1996 with the triumphant headline "Finally We're Winning the War Against Crime. Here's Why." In large part because New York was the star city of the crime drop, the "broken windows" approach was adopted in city after city. Bratton subsequently left New York to head up the LAPD, where he also put his methods to work. He published a best-selling memoir with the immodest title *Turnaround: How America's Top Cop Reversed the Crime Epidemic.*

While the actual role that "broken windows" policing played in the dramatic drop in crime is still hard to disentangle (about which more in a moment), one thing is certain: its implementation fundamentally and permanently altered the city in two distinct, indelible ways. First, it completely changed the mise-en-scène of city life, erasing the seediness that colored my youth. As the Giuliani era hit full bloom, you would hear cheery pronouncements from out-of-town visitors about how transformed Manhattan was: *So clean! So accessible! So much more inviting!*

Second, "broken windows" as a philosophy of urban governance altered the administration of justice in New York City. Issa Kohler-Hausmann, who's done some of the most thorough empirical work on New York City's "quality of life" arrests, notes that while arrests for low-level offenses skyrocketed, the actual rate of criminal convictions dropped. She argues that "broken windows" actually created a parallel court system, with an altogether different set of goals.

> Misdemeanor justice in New York City has largely abandoned what I call the adjudicative model of criminal law administration—concerned with adjudicating guilt and punishment in specific cases—and instead operates under what I call the managerial model—concerned with managing people over time through engagement with the criminal justice system over time.

In other words, New York constructed an entire new judicial system around low-level offenses. The goal of this system is not to figure out if the person in question committed a crime but to sort city residents according to their obedience and orderliness. So expansive is this system of misdemeanor sorting that in a city that's 80 percent less violent than it was two decades ago, the NYPD makes thousands of arrests a year of people who are doing things like selling M&Ms

on the subway. Similar explosions of small-infraction misdemeanor citations, and summons happened across the country, from New York to Chicago to Los Angeles to Ferguson.

This system of order maintenance, in which unruly citizens are marked and sorted, in which seediness is kept at bay, so that the Nation can stay pristine and inviting, confers tremendous benefits, wealth, and comfort on some and widespread harassment and misery on others.

New York went from rundown and dangerous to glossy and glamorous, and the transformation unleashed a geyser of cash. Between 1991 and 2015 the number of visitors to the city more than doubled, from 29 million to 58 million. The amount those visitors spent annually quadrupled from $10 billion to $40 billion.

Colleges and universities across the city saw an application boom, just one small indication of how the city's ebbing "seediness" conferred tangible, material economic benefits on its institutions and businesses. But more than anything, the drop in crime and the palpable decline in disorder produced one of the greatest increases in real estate value in American history.

I SAW IT HAPPEN firsthand.

Every day from seventh grade until I graduated high school, I rode an express bus from the Bronx down to my school on the Upper East Side. The route passed through Harlem, one of New York's most legendary neighborhoods. Once upon a time Harlem was affluent, an uptown proto-suburb, away from the crowds, noise, and stench of nineteenth-century downtown Manhattan. Its opulence in certain quarters persisted into the twentieth century as it became the intellectual and artistic capital of black life in America.

By 1991, when I started passing through Harlem, decades of government policy had crowded it with housing projects, while starving it of capital through redlining. But the beauty of Harlem was always there even amid the physical disintegration that comes with poverty.

At 125th Street, Fifth Avenue dead-ends at Marcus Garvey Park, a lovely eight-square-block patch of green with a swimming pool and recreation center, ringed on all sides by stately brownstones built just after 1900. In my youth, the buildings were derelict and almost all abandoned, and the park was, well, seedy. A halfway house stood on an adjacent block. But I was taken with what a staggeringly lovely spot it was. I used to dream of that park and those stately buildings peering out over it.

Fast-forward to 2016, and one of the brownstones on the western border of the park is listed for $5 million. "Mount Morris Park West is one of the most sought after blocks if not the most sought after block in prime Harlem!!!," exclaims the listing, describing it as

> situated on a quiet residential area, but it is also surrounded by various shopping, great restaurants, and

transportation. Soon to be finished Whole Foods
around the corner on 125th and Lenox; furthermore
local restaurants include celeb chef Marcus Samuel-
son's Red Rooster, as well as Corner Social, Cheri,
Maison Harlem, Chez Lucienne, and many more.

Just around the block from that house, on the south side
of Marcus Garvey Park, stands a luxury high-rise, Fifth on
the Park, built in 2007. A three-bedroom apartment goes for
about $2.4 million. You can't help but notice that the official
real estate listing calls Marcus Garvey Park by its original,
decidedly less black-separatist name, Mount Morris Park.

For so long change had gone in one direction: toward
flight, ruin, and entropy. Then the great crime wave subsided, and the tide reversed. In many of the places where
real estate prices have skyrocketed, from Harlem to Bedford-
Stuyvesant in Brooklyn, little has changed in the neighborhood's actual fundamentals. Like those buildings along
the park, these places always featured proximity to subways,
beautiful architecture, and tree-lined streets, and they have
been, for decades, predominantly black and brown neighborhoods. The only thing that made them cheap was the self-
fulfilling financial logic of the ghetto: no money was to be
made in improving the place because only poor people were
going to live there.

It wasn't the race of the residents of these neighborhoods
that changed first but the levels of crime and danger and
(perhaps even more importantly) the perception of same.

And with that change in perception, access to capital opened dramatically. Getting a loan for a brownstone in, say, Bed-Stuy in the mid-1960s had been difficult if not impossible. In the Bronx, capital was so scarce that an entire system of government programs and nonprofits was created to funnel money into building renovations and improvements. (I worked summer jobs at one of these organizations, the University Neighborhood Housing Program.)

That chapter of urban history now feels very remote. Today interest rates are low, cash is cheap, prices are going up, and the holders of great wealth—banks, hedge funds, individual rich people—are looking to invest in New York real estate. The sheer amount of real estate wealth created in the city in the last twenty years is staggering to contemplate. At the beginning of 1998, according to data from Zillow, the total value of all New York City residential real estate was about $283 billion (adjusted for inflation). By April 2014, that value had more than tripled to $935 billion. That's $650 billion in *just* residential real estate value created in less than two decades.

New York is the place where crime dropped the most, and where the cumulative value of real estate almost certainly exploded with the biggest boom. But city after city has experienced versions of the same thing: drops in crime, spikes in real estate prices, and a process of gentrification that has pushed up rents for poor and working-class people, creating a nationwide affordability crisis. In 1984 poor Americans spent 35 percent of their income on rent. By 2014 that was 41 percent, with fully half of renters below the poverty line spending most of their total income to keep a roof over their head.

In *Evicted*, Matthew Desmond shows a snapshot of how this played out in one American city, Milwaukee. Due to rising rents, the poor are constantly behind on their bills, their homes are contingent on the generosity of their landlords, and they move from apartment to apartment in a state of constant desperate disruption.

From Milwaukee to New York, the process of real estate wealth creation has often come at the direct expense of the city's poor. "Whatever positive effects the demographic shifts in Brooklyn are creating," Raphael Ruttenberg, who works as a tenants' lawyer in the borough, tells me, "the devastation has been profound. The poor of the city are being crushed under the wheel of progress. Entire neighborhoods are being effectively cleansed of the working poor who have been there for decades."

Ruttenberg gave me an example of how this works in practice, in a building in the far eastern reaches of Brooklyn, a bleeding-edge frontier in the city's gentrification map. The neighborhood is firmly in the Colony now, but not for long if its new owners have their way. In one building he represents, the landlords who bought the place in 2014 offered the tenants, all black and Hispanic, $10,000 to leave. When most balked ($10,000 sounds like a lot, but it doesn't go far in the Brooklyn rental market), the landlords lowered the buyout fee to $4,000. Then as Ruttenberg described it to me:

The landlord later told the remaining tenants that
they'd better take the (now $4,000) buyout offer,
because he was planning to renovate the vacant
apartments, which he threatened would be hazard-
ous to the health of the remaining tenants' young
children. The renovations seem designed explicitly
to harass the tenants, including knocking down
parts of the ceiling in one apartment. There is dust
and debris throughout the building, and holes and
cracks in all the walls. The renovations may have
even made the building structurally unsound. And
the landlord has flouted stop-work orders from the
Department of Buildings to continue his harassment
by construction.

It's not just this one building—stories like this are commonplace throughout the borough. "Brooklyn is in the
midst of a gold rush," Ruttenberg says, "and true to the Wild
West metaphor, there is plenty of illegal activity and very
little policing happening."

I laughed when he said that. Of course, there's a whole lot
of policing happening in those neighborhoods—just not of
this particular kind of activity.

The signature achievement of the reign of order is that a
person can live in the Nation and never know what hardship
may befall the Colony. "I like to tell people that there is a
war going on," Ruttenberg says, "which most of us in New
York are dimly aware of."

Maintaining ignorance of life in the Colony was a good deal harder in the New York of my youth, when disorder imposed itself on you. The problems of the poor tugged at your attention. Today new wealth created in the "revitalized," "reborn" American metropolis has put that unpleasantness out of view. An endless cultural conversation swirls about the lives of the young, highly educated citizens of America's hip urban neighborhoods. TV shows and articles discuss what they like and don't like, where they eat and don't eat. The city as an entity now means a different thing entirely. *Fort Apache* has given way to *Girls*.

All the while, deep poverty, routine lethal violence, and epidemic levels of trauma persist in the Colony. There citizens find themselves pushed further toward the geographical margins, squeezed both by the punishing arithmetic of poverty and by the ceaseless surveillance of a police force tasked with corralling that poverty and keeping order in places the Nation has not yet annexed.

In 1997 I went to college, then moved to Chicago and D.C., and when I'd come back to visit New York, I found the old borders had been erased. White people were venturing everywhere! On my train rides from Manhattan back uptown to my parents' house in the Bronx, I used to have a trick that would always ensure me a seat. I'd find a white person and stand right in front of them, certain they'd get off the train before Harlem and Washington Heights. But now my method no longer worked so well. I'd lurk over some white guy with a backpack, sneakers, and a paperback and would be shocked when he didn't get off until 181st Street.

On the weekend nights when I visited the city, my friends who lived in the new New York would take me out to bars in Bushwick and Alphabet City, precincts that had once been part of the Colony but were now being absorbed into the Nation. For the relatively affluent, the hip, the privileged, the young and white and restless, the borders of the city had massively expanded. New York had essentially doubled in size! And in a place as crowded as this metropolis, the promise of more space was enticing. Those years of Rudy Giuliani and then Michael Bloomberg were marked by a kind of frontier euphoria among a certain (quite influential) set of New Yorkers. And for those less adventurous, it meant they could drop the cloak of white fear.

I cast it aside as well. I can't remember when exactly, but I have distinct snapshot memories of moments in New York, walking around some neighborhood that might have been a foreign land in my youth and experiencing the sense of freedom that came with no longer attuning myself to every single last little bit of perceptual stimulus. A sense of being present fully and gloriously where I was, without looking over my shoulder.

I live in this city now, again, after being away for a long time. Our neighborhood is quiet, just a few blocks from the leafy parkside apartment where I last called the cops. There's no graffiti on the trains, and no homeless on the streets where we live. There are cheese shops and yoga studios and farmers' markets and playgrounds. For the small percentage of New Yorkers rich enough to enjoy it, life in the city has never been better. It's still hard in its own bracing way, but it's all so orderly now.

It's also a heck of a lot safer and not just for people who live in the more rarified blocks of the Nation. Defenders of the "broken windows" approach, who include former NYPD commissioners Bratton and Ray Kelly, former mayor Giuliani, and the current liberal mayor Bill DeBlasio, argue that it was the central, key factor in the historic drop in crime, and as such its own kind of civil rights victory. Because people of color, particularly poor black city residents, were the most common victims of crime, and because they were the greatest beneficiaries of crime's decline, the argument goes, all of the increased enforcement was actually *on their behalf*.

President Bill Clinton's 1994 crime bill put many more cops on the street under an explicit "broken windows" theory of order and deterrence. In the spring of 2016 he defended that law to a Black Lives Matter heckler this way: "Because of that [crime] bill we had a 25-year low in crime, a 33-year low in the murder rate, and listen to this, because of that and the background-check law, we had a 46-year low in the deaths of people by gun violence," he said. "*And who do you think those lives were that mattered? Whose lives were saved that mattered?*"

But it's deeply unclear that this is true. Crime started falling before the crime bill was passed, and also before Rudy Giuliani was elected and Bill Bratton installed.

Why? We have no idea.

THE DROP IN CRIME in the United States from 1992 through today is one of the most stunning statistical and sociological mysteries of our time. A number of things are distinctive about it. First, crime dropped across all categories, from larceny to assaults to rape and murder. It dropped across all geographic areas, from the Deep South up to Maine. It dropped in rural areas, in midsize cities, and in big ones. It dropped in places with lots of racial diversity and in places with almost none. Perhaps most perplexing, it dropped in good economic times and in bad. You'd expect that in the wake of recession and economic crisis, at least certain categories of crime—property crimes, for example—would spike. But during both the relatively mild recession of 2001 and the historically awful Great Recession of 2007–9, even property crimes continued their decline.

As you might expect, this apparent victory over crime has a million self-proclaimed fathers. Literally dozens of theories claim to explain what "caused it," but none of them definitive. Simple demographics played a large role: The baby boom meant that beginning in the late 1960s, a huge number of men entered into their peak crime-committing years. And indeed, crime spikes in developed nations (Canada among others) followed a similar trajectory (though not quite as pronounced as in the United States).

Mass incarceration also played some role in reducing crime. A society that put, say, every man aged 18 to 24 under carceral supervision could expect to see a reduction in violent crime, since that population commits a disproportionate amount of it. We also understand that that would be a tyrannical, indefensible slave state, but in large swaths of black and brown America, that's not too far from what has happened.

But the best research seems to indicate that while the initial increase in incarceration did have an effect on crime reduction in the 1980s, the two million more put behind bars thereafter did nothing to further reduce crime. And the states that have moved most swiftly to reduce prison populations haven't seen a crime bump.

Certain tantalizing theories on the drop in crime have literally nothing at all to do with policing, crime, or even economics. For instance, some public health experts argue (persuasively) that the postwar car boom dramatically increased the amount of lead in the atmosphere; then with the elimination of lead in gasoline and paint, crime rates fell. According to proponents of this theory, the varying levels of environmental lead alone accounts for nearly all of the boom and bust in America's postwar crime rates.

Another explanation involves the changing structure of the drug war and drug markets. The launch of the War on Drugs in 1971 drove an ever-burgeoning black market worth billions of dollars that played, according to those who have studied the matter, a significant role in the rise in crime. In the late 1980s, as crack flowed into America's poor, urban neighborhoods, it unsettled existing markets, creating new winners and losers. Violence exploded over turf and market control. During the Crack Years of the mid-1980s to mid-

1990s, homicide rates more than doubled for black boys aged 14 to 17 and nearly doubled for black men aged 18 to 24.

As for "broken windows" policing, its connection to the crime decline is murky. Legal scholars Bernard Harcourt and Jens Ludwig tracked different populations in five different cities and found "no support for a simple first-order disorder-crime relationship as hypothesized by Wilson and Kelling, nor for the proposition that 'broken windows' policing is the optimal use of scarce law enforcement resources."

But recent research has lent a bit more credence to the basic causal theory about the relationship between crime and disorder. A 2015 meta-analysis of thirty different studies of "disorder policing" found that such strategies "are associated with an overall statistically significant, modest crime reduction effect." But it also concludes that "aggressive order maintenance strategies that target individual disorderly behaviors do not generate significant crime reductions."

In short, despite reams of literature on the topic, we simply have reached no broad-based consensus about what "caused" the crime decline. "If you take every paper that says this factor explains x percentage of the crime drop," jokes law professor John Pfaff, who studies mass incarceration, "and add them up, you get 250 percent. That's a huge red flag."

The crime drop was almost certainly the result of a dynamic combination of factors. But in the absence of a rock-solid case for one specific explanation, anyone with a pet policy can plausibly claim it was that policy that did the trick. And obviously those who worked in law enforcement during the period have every incentive, both political and psychological, to argue that their innovations, reforms, and sustained methodological improvements should get the credit.

Elected officials, for their part, have powerful incentives not to alter the machinery, not to do anything that might draw too much attention. Since no one actually knows why crime is down (though many think they do), the cargo cult of white fear requires certain rituals be maintained, and when they are flouted, a visceral collective anxiety results, stoked unfailingly by demagogues. Everyone tasked with keeping crime from returning has developed deeply held, near-religious beliefs about What Works. We are farmers begging the Gods to keep the drought away; we will give them what they want, if they will spare us their wrath.

Any political momentum to reduce mass incarceration, strengthen police accountability, and rethink our approach to justice rests on the continuation of the oh-so-delicate status quo, in which crime continues at historic lows. But what happens when that changes? In Baltimore, which experienced a horrific surge in murder and violent crime after Freddie Gray, the apparent vengeance of the crime gods ripped the entire city's political order apart. That same fate hangs over any politician who would take bold steps toward decolonization and integration, if such steps also correspond with an increase in crime. Just ask New York's mayor.

By the time Bill DeBlasio took office, "stop and frisk" had become a widely deployed tool under Ray Kelly, who helmed the NYPD under Mayor Bloomberg.* In Bloomberg's final years, grassroots activists exerted increasing political pressure against the policy, then were joined by politicians representing the millions of the city's black and Latino residents who were being robbed of their constitutional freedoms. As a result, "stop and frisk" started to decline, and DeBlasio made ending it one of the signatures of his campaign. When a federal judge ruled its implementation in New York unconstitutional, DeBlasio did not appeal.

Kelly and the police union fought like mad to preserve the practice, warning in increasingly dire, apocalyptic terms of the hell to which the city would return if random young black and brown men could no longer be detained routinely on a whim for no discernible reason. *We will anger the crime gods!* they practically shouted. *We shall see drought for a thousand years!*

But the drought never came, and the vengeance never arrived. The numbers are in. They show essentially zero relationship between "stop and frisk" and crime in the city. But the superstitions live on in other forms.

A few months after the protests following Mike Brown's death in Ferguson, St. Louis police chief Sam Dotson spoke of what he called a "Ferguson effect": cops were now demor-

---

* Like Bill Bratton under DeBlasio, Ray Kelly had been on his second tour of duty under Bloomberg. Even the fact that mayors are reluctant to appoint new people to the job shows how powerfully politicians avoid risk in managing crime in New York.

alized, hesitant, and exhausted, he said, while the "criminal element" was feeling empowered by the environment.

In 2015 the conservative pundit Heather Mac Donald wrote an op-ed for the *Wall Street Journal* asserting that the Ferguson effect had gone national, that cops around the country were now so afraid of protest and criticism they'd stopped doing their jobs, and as a result a "new national crime wave" was beginning to crest. Before you knew it, the "Ferguson effect" became a known phenomenon, accepted by cops, prosecutors, mayors, pundits and others as gospel truth. The moment any crime happened anywhere, local tabloids and national right-wing media ran stories about the "Ferguson effect." Even Chicago mayor Rahm Emanuel, a Democrat, said that police were now so terrified of the onslaught of public scrutiny brought about by cell phone videos and Black Lives Matter protests, they had been reduced to a "fetal" position.

As a hypothesis, the "Ferguson effect" was, at least in a national sense, way out ahead of what the data could plausibly show. It was a thesis in search of data, identified before anything definitive had been concluded. (Later, data would show that homicides in 2015 had their biggest jump since 1971, driven mostly by a few major cities.) Under Mayor DeBlasio, crime in New York is at a historic low, despite the 70 percent decrease in "stop and frisk" encounters between 2011 and 2015.

Nonetheless the mayors and pundits charged ahead. *This is what happens when you question the cops,* they argued, *and when you tug on the strings of the tough-on-crime consensus. The entire* *thing unravels, and we find ourselves hurled down back into the bad old days of rampant violence and criminality. The jungle returns.* That's precisely the warning that foes of Mayor DeBlasio had been offering since before he was elected. And now with each shooting, stabbing, and gruesome crime in the city, they pointed to it as the moment when everything slips back, when all the progress is forfeited and constant anxiety returns.*

If I'm entirely honest with myself, I have to admit that I, too, fear the bad old days' return. I enjoy the orderliness of the current city. I own a home. I have kids. I don't want them encountering addicts on the corner. I don't want a lot of disorder on the streets.

And here is the awful implication of this seemingly innocent desire for order: people like me who reside in the Nation enjoy the benefits of increased real estate values, tranquil urban streets, and poverty quarantined out of view. We directly, materially, personally benefit from the status quo, no matter what awful costs it imposes on those in the Colony. This is the dark magic of the politics of order: fear lurks in the hearts of the Nation's citizens that if the Colony were ever liberated, if the police were withdrawn and rights restored, life in the Nation might grow much, much worse. Crime, it turns out, is more easily subdued than fear.

* When, in 2015, a microtrend of topless, painted women started charging tourists in Times Square to take photos with them, the voices of reaction in the city cried out: *Here we go again. The bad old days are back!* (The mayor quietly moved to get rid of the women.)

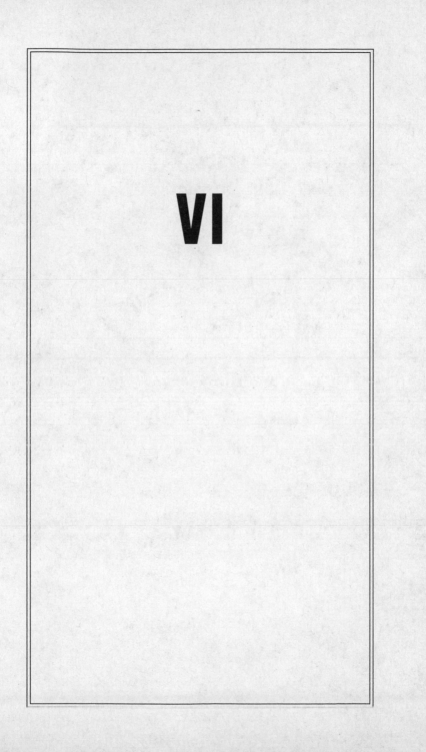

VI

America is a wrathful land. Americans like to humiliate wrongdoers. We like to heap marks of shame upon them, to watch them groan and writhe beneath their sins, as far back as the scarlet letter and the stocks. We like, in short, to punish. It makes us feel good. By every conceivable metric—prosecutions, duration of sentences, conditions of imprisonment—the United States is by far the most punitive rich democracy. No one else really comes close.

And we are, of course, the only rich democracy that hands out the ultimate punishment: death. Year after year, when the dead around the world have been tallied, the beheadings and the hangings and firing squads and lethal injections, we join Iran, Iraq, Saudi Arabia, Jordan, Somalia, North Korea, and China.

This isn't simply a manifestation of the democratic desires

of Americans, our collective desire to see "them" pay. Surprisingly, public opinion data from Europe shows fairly strong popular support for the death penalty, despite the fact that the practice is banned in the EU. In Britain 50 percent support the death penalty. In France it's 45 percent.

Perhaps this shouldn't be surprising. Bloodlust from the crowd is a common trait; every country on earth has experienced some form of it. In a democracy, the politics of crime present the possibility of vigilantism by other means. Imagine a referendum, Pontius Pilate style, for every person convicted of, say, child molestation. How many would vote for death? We insulate criminal procedure from direct democracy precisely because of the corrupting force of the will of the people. We don't give child molesters death sentences, but that's not because such a sentence wouldn't meet, under the right conditions, with majority approval.

Part of what sets Europe apart in this respect is the degree to which its criminal justice system operates free from democratic input. The United States is more or less the only advanced democracy that *elects* its prosecutors. As the legal scholar William Stuntz points out, those electorates often draw from an entire county, which includes urban and suburban areas, so that predominantly white, middle-class-to-affluent suburban voters are choosing who will prosecute the largely poor black people arrested by the police. The idea of electing prosecutors, as we do in the United States, strikes most European jurists as sheer madness. In almost all cases, the continental criminal justice system is far more bureaucratic, more insulated from electoral politics than our own.

But there's a philosophical difference, too. In 2003 law professor James Whitman laid out an argument for why the U.S. criminal justice system compares so poorly to those of continental Europe—France and Germany specifically. For most of his analysis, Whitman explicitly puts race to one side (about which more in a moment), but in looking at the development of the continental system versus the U.S. system, he comes to a surprising and compelling conclusion: that it is the strong anti-aristocratic strain in the American legal tradition that has made our punishment system so remorseless and harsh.

In the German and French systems, he explains, punishment long existed along two separate tracks: degradation and humiliation for low-status prisoners and relative comfort and hospitality for high-status ones. The United States, on the other hand, maintained a more egalitarian ethos of punishment (for white people, anyway). Since the American Revolution, we viewed punishment as a great equalizer; no special kinds of punishment was reserved for lords and for peasants. Thus the system of punishment that developed found equality in a race to the bottom: everyone got punished harshly as an expression of a core belief that no man stands above another.

In Europe, as it democratized over time, the move was to push everyone into the category once reserved for the nobles: the sphere of humane treatment was widened until

it included everyone. "Over the course of the last two centuries," Whitman writes, "in both Germany and France,
and indeed throughout the continent of Europe, the
high-status punishments have slowly driven the low-status
punishments out. . . . These countries are the scene of a
leveling-up egalitarianism—an egalitarianism whose aim
is to raise every member of society up in social status."

The United States, which never had a separate, formal
aristocratic form of justice and punishment, one embedded in deference to the perpetrator's core humanity, has,
instead, been subject to the opposite push:

> Where nineteenth-century continental Europeans
> slowly began to generalize high-status treatment,
> nineteenth-century Americans moved strongly to
> abolish high-status treatment. From a very early
> date, Americans showed instead, at least sporadi-
> cally, a typical tendency to generalize norms of *low*-
> status treatment—to level down.

Whitman traces the historical currents that produced
these twin impulses, but part of what made "leveling up"
possible on the continent was a solidarity that flourished
in postwar Europe, binding societies with a shared ethnic-
ity and language. The person you may feel an impulse to
degrade is your fellow Frenchman, after all.

In the United States, the bulk of the populace cleaves
apart perpetrators and victims, attributing criminals to one

racial group and victims to another. The statistics don't bear out this division—thanks in no small part to the pervasive segregation of American life, almost all crime in the United States is committed intraracially. White people are most likely to be victimized by other white people, black people are most likely to fall victim to other black people.

But this is not the way crime is communicated publicly. It is communicated in the language of war: with the enemy criminals on one side, and victims on the other. And so when we speak of the politics of crime over the last three decades, we are speaking, almost without exception, of the politics of crime victimization. Politicians in their stump speeches tell hagiographies of victims and vilify the perpetrators. The last several decades have seen a concerted movement on behalf of victims to carve out a larger role in the criminal justice system, instituting victim impact statements, for instance. In many ways this has been salutary, as the trauma of violence for victims and survivors is profound and long-lasting, and the criminal justice system, to this day, still fails to adequately support them.

But a crime discourse that focuses on the evil of the acts has ruinous political consequences, especially for any attempt to create a system that values the humanity of the people who commit crimes.

George H. W. Bush's 1988 presidential campaign ran an infamous ad about an incarcerated black man, Willie Horton, who participated in a weekend furlough program, escaped, and then went on to rape and murder. With its grainy photo of Horton, it was effective because it spoke to potential voters who could imagine themselves as his victim. *This scary black man might come and find you or someone you love and kill them. Do you want to vote for the candidate who would let someone like that out on the loose?*

But tens of thousands of other people participated in similar furlough programs across the country and never committed any kind of infraction. After Horton was apprehended, a group of his fellow lifers in a Massachusetts prison wrote to legislators pleading with them not to apply the lesson too broadly. "We ask that you treat [Horton's] case as it is, which is an individual case and does not and should not reflect on the . . . people who have accepted the responsibility . . . and are serving their time in a very positive and productive manner."

In fact, during the 1980s every single U.S. state had some kind of furlough program. California ran a furlough program, which had also been in operation years earlier under Governor Ronald Reagan. After a prisoner on furlough committed a murder, Reagan defended the program, saying, "More than 20,000 already have these passes, and this was the only case of this kind, the only murder." Reagan even bragged about California "leading the nation in rehabilitation. . . . Obviously you can't be perfect."

Any criminal justice system imposes costs not just on the perpetrators of crime but on their friends, family, and loved ones. Those costs are particularly acute for children who suffer trauma from absent parental figures. In a social context in which voters and the state understand criminals to disproportionately come from certain areas and segments of society, the vast majority of people can safely ignore those costs, because they are borne by those out of view. A politician can say "get tough on crime," and the majority of voters won't worry that it's their neighbor's kid who's going to grow up without a father because he's doing ten years.

Crime in America is associated with the lower classes, the ghetto, the others, the Colony. But what would the politics of crime look like in a place where people worried not only about victimization but *also* about the costs of overly punitive policing and prosecution? What kind of justice system would exist in a setting in which each member of society were actually valued as a full human with tremendous potential, even if he or she committed a crime, or hurt someone, or broke the community's norms and were held accountable? What would it look like to have a system where, behind the veil of ignorance, every member had an equal chance to end up as perpetrator or victim? What would a criminal justice system for the elite look like? How would people with power and privilege and resources and influence choose to collectively police themselves if given the ability?

WE DON'T HAVE TO speculate; hundreds of examples are operating right now across every single state of the union.

I speak, of course, of elite four-year colleges and universities, public and private. I was fortunate enough to attend one of them, Brown University in Providence, Rhode Island, but the same basic factors apply everywhere from the University of Southern California to the University of Wisconsin at Madison to the University of North Carolina at Chapel Hill to New York University.

All these schools and hundreds of others draw their student bodies disproportionately from upper echelons of society, and they are places where parents and administrators outright expect students to engage in illicit behaviors.

Almost all campuses have some kind of internal justice system, composed of both campus police and extensive disciplinary codes and procedures for adjudication, appeal, and punishment. When I was eighteen, I found the legal status of the Brown campus police deeply unclear: Were they just private security guards with a fancier name? Did they have the cover of law? I recall seeing them once or twice actually placing someone under arrest and wondering, *Can they do that?*

The answer is yes. Brown University's department of public safety "is a fully-accredited police department," whose eighty-five members are "licensed as RI Special Police Officers" and "are authorized to enforce state statutes and university rules and regulations."

But having had interactions with both the Brown University Police and the actual Providence Police, I can tell you why we used to call Brown cops "Four Point Nines": because they weren't quite Five-Oh.

I remember one night during the glorious week between

the end of finals and commencement weekend, when a small group of students had stuck around to work odd jobs or (in my case) rehearse for plays that would be performed during the big weekend when the campus lights up with the prideful glow of thousands of parents.

Having no studying to do or classes to attend, we devoted the evenings to partying—in this case, in a cinder block suite in a dorm building on campus that had (somewhat famously) been designed in the late 1960s during waves of campus unrest to be efficiently penetrated by cops if the situation called for it. Since the building was largely unoccupied, we'd spread our stuff throughout the suite. Sitting on the grungy-carpeted floor of the common room, we passed around a pipe with a stoner pal in town visiting from another school, getting high and blasting vintage hip hop.

Suddenly and silently a Brown police officer appeared in the room. The music was loud, and we were so stoned, I have no idea how long he was standing there before we noticed him. The air was so thick with pot smoke—it must've made his eyes water. Eventually we realized he was there, and we looked up. I think it was my stoner friend who had the pipe in his hand, mid-pull.

The cop was young, white, and fresh faced. There was a long pregnant pause, as the room fell silent but for the song on the stereo.

"Hey," he finally said, "is that Eric B. and Rakim?"

"Yup," my friend said.

"Love this album," he said.

We all nodded in vigorous agreement.

"We're just going through the dorms, since it's commencement week, making sure everything's cool. You guys cool?"

"We're cool."

"Okay, have a good night." And he was gone.

A moment of hysterical laughter and deep breaths, and then back to illicit activity and foolish dorm room conversation.

It is possible, I suppose, that had we been in off-campus housing and had a Providence cop shown up on a call only to encounter us smoking pot in the living room, he would've done the same thing. I mean, cops do look the other way on occasion. Their authority in the moment of interaction is near-absolute: they can be merciful or vengeful. But I'd bet anything that things would've turned out quite a bit differently.

Which is the point. Would any parent pay $50,000 a year to send their kid to a place where it was likely, or even possible, they'd pick up a criminal record for smoking pot? Particularly the affluent, powerful influential parents who send their kids to schools like Brown? I sure as hell wouldn't.

That's because elite four-year schools are understood by almost everyone involved in them—parents, students, faculty, administrators—as places where young adults act out, experiment, and violate rules in all kinds of ways. And that's more or less okay, or even more than okay; sometimes it's encouraged. Rebellion is part of the experience: *Oh, the fun we had, the wild hijinks we were up to!*

The modern American bourgeoisie has its own institutionalized version of the Rumspringa, which suspends the highly routinized and proscribed behavioral rules of affluent American life so that young adults can purge the wildness from their systems before becoming orderly, boring, and high-achieving professionals.

To borrow the framework of Kelling and Wilson, a fair amount of *disorder* prevails on a modern college campus. It is, by and large, well hidden, which means there aren't any actual broken windows (at least not on campus; off-campus housing is another story). But walk into any dorm, and you will find absolute chaos and disorder. And the lives of the citizens of these mini-states are disordered as well, particularly as compared to the lives most of them will lead once they are members of the professional classes.

If you took a lot of this behavior out of the Nation and put it in the Colony—say, out of Harvard Yard and into a big city housing project—it would provide the material for dozens of articles on the pathologies of poverty that hold back poor people of color. People sleep all day; they engage in loud, frequent relationship dramas while having numerous different sexual partners; and they get into drunken arguments and brawls and consume ungodly amounts of controlled substances.

To be fair, these extremely liberal norms of tolerance can have their own negative consequences. In my time at Brown, numerous friends and people in my social circle fell victim to alcoholism and drug addiction, not to mention acute depression.

Booze and pot were omnipresent. But other harder drugs were also around, though they tended to lurk at the edges. Some kind of vague social taboo (combined with expense) kept people from busting out coke or heroin at a party, although at other schools where my friends attended (and which I visited), that taboo definitely did not obtain.

An acquaintance I'll call E attended such a school, another elite private college in the Northeast, where the attitude toward drugs and alcohol was notoriously and famously lax. "My first year there, there was a new president being inaugurated on the same day as this kind of festival where everyone trips on acid. There was an outdoor space with four hundred kids tripping on acid. You could actually see the president's inauguration, and the two existed side by side."

E and his friends started doing more and harder drugs. "You had a lot of eighteen-, nineteen-year-olds with a lot of money. It was crazy the amount of drugs. Out of my group of friends, most of us ended up doing heroin, and one of my best friends died of an overdose a few years out."

By junior year, E was doing heroin consistently, and after he graduated, he spent six months in New York as an addict with a hundred-dollar-a-day habit. Today he's a successful father and husband working in education. E's very clear not to blame anyone else for his addiction, but in retrospect he can't bring himself to quite endorse his alma mater's posture of extreme tolerance. "It's like the worst of progressive education. It was an abdication of your responsibility.

I never saw campus police do anything about drugs or the administration or anybody."

If colleges and universities are relatively permissive on drugs (and obviously that level of tolerance varies widely), it's because they are for all intents and purposes mini-states, with their very own internal justice systems. Alexandra Brodsky, who co-founded Know Your IX, a student-run anti-violence organization, says there's a good reason for this. "I'm a big believer in schools handling discipline internally. . . . You have a self-selecting community with its own norms, some ways more permissive [drugs] and in some ways stricter [plagiarism]. . . . The big danger is things being referred to police automatically."

It's those community norms that Kelling and Wilson celebrate, but in the case of campuses, the in-groups and out-groups are far clearer than in high-crime neighborhoods. The same goes (to a certain extent) for what those community norms are. A certain amount of wildness is expected, and you might even find some drunkards breaking the occasional window.

WHEN I WAS TWENTY-FIVE, I spent a few months in Madison working for the League of Conservation Voters as a field organizer trying to get John Kerry elected.* I was kindly offered free lodging in the basement of a lovely home on

* I hasten to add that he did win Wisconsin that year, 2004.

Madison's west side. I loved the town, with its combination of big university culture and state capital political intrigue. It was charming and livable in every respect, and as summer turned into fall, football season arrived, and the Badgers had a pretty good team that year.

Now, Brown had had a whole lot of drug use and drinking and partying, but it was not a Big Ten football school with a tradition of officially sanctioned, campus-wide bacchanals each weekend. Nothing I'd seen during my college years quite prepared me for the sheer insanity of a big football program home game. Tens upon tens of thousands of people, of all ages, were shit-faced drunk. Frat row was in a state of debaucherous pandemonium, with dozens of students passed out on lawns and outdoor couches, amid no small amount of vomit, urine, and broken bottles. I mean, it was fun, I guess. Or at least it looked like it would be fun if you were a participant, if you woke up and started pounding beers and found yourself, dressed in red, gleefully among the throng. I'm sure it was amazing.

But I was working on the weekends, riding my bike through the crowds, and I couldn't but help feel alienated from the entire enterprise. I also couldn't help but imagine how this scene would play out if the crowds weren't overwhelmingly white. I mean, would all this (mostly harmless) mayhem meet with such enthusiastic tolerance if it were a hundred thousand drunk-as-hell black folks streaming through downtown Madison? Something tells me, no chance.

The couple I was staying with had season tickets to the

games, and while they rolled their eyes a touch at some of the excesses, they were part of a community, and they understood and embraced that this was a community ritual, a norm collectively arrived at. So they did not panic about the absolute carnival of disorder that game day represented. It was, in its own way, orderly disorder. Which is one way of describing four years at college.

Of course, it's not always that easy. Large universities tend to exist not simply behind fortressed walls but over a large area that mixes official campus buildings, unofficial parts of the school (houses and apartments rented by students), and residences where nonstudents live: the "decent folk," as Kelling and Wilson call them.

And if you are raising your family in the neighborhood of a large, intoxicated student body, you probably wish you could somehow get a little "broken windows" policing. Sarah Koenig, a producer for *This American Life* and *Serial*, documented the trials of her family living in a house in State College, Pennsylvania. She showed how onerous it was to be constantly dealing with drunken young people peeing on your lawn, pulling traffic signs out of the ground, and carousing at all hours of the night.

By and large, though, campus police and college towns' police departments are not guided by the "broken windows" ethos; if they were, State College, Pennsylvania, Madison, Wisconsin, Bloomington, Indiana, and Boulder, Colorado, would all be police states. I've corresponded and talked to dozens of people about their experiences with campus cops, and there are certainly examples of cruelty and harshness, even the kinds of horrifying fatal shootings of unarmed students that have made headlines. As with any job where someone has a badge and authority over other people, there are more than a few sadistic assholes who get off on ordering people around.

At some schools the division of labor between benign pastoral care for unruly drunken teenagers and actual public safety is institutionalized with two different kinds of forces. At Johns Hopkins there are, a junior told me:

> the HopCops, who don neon yellow jackets, and the Campus Security, who wear policeman-like uniforms. The HopCops exist solely for student safety and are incredibly progressive. They don't care if you're hammered or high or anything as long as you're not hurting anyone. One of them caught me smoking MJ on top of a campus building and told me it was his favorite spot too and to make sure that none of the Campus Security saw me: pretty chill. The Security, on the other hand, are killjoys, often raiding the quads to confiscate alcohol on sunny days. I was ambushed by one after he watched me and a buddy depart a liquor store and head to the dorms. He was waiting at the elevator and told me he saw everything and to take the beer elsewhere.

You can't help but notice here that even the harsher force doesn't write a ticket or make an arrest for underage drinking. But that's not necessarily how those outside the campus community encounter those same officers.

Campus police stand as watchmen for the assorted hijinks of rebellious and often out-of-control young adults. They break up parties and make sure no one gets hurt, as opposed to bringing the hammer of law and order down on every drunk underage student they encounter. That is the role they play in the campus community. But they are also there to keep the outside world at bay. They are sentries who stand on the wall.

Many students of color have told me they found their race automatically led campus cops to think they were outsiders rather than members of the community. Almost every black and brown student, it seems, has a story about being profiled by campus cops as infiltrators. In 2004 at William and Mary, where Dani Perea went to school, she and her friend, who is black, were studying in the library and laughing at something when a

> campus cop materialized at our table and asked if we were guests of the college. . . . He told us we weren't supposed to be there unless we were guests of the college. . . . He said something like, "You're going to be in trouble if you don't tell me what you're doing here." . . . My friend pulled out her lanyard with her student ID and showed it to him and told him that we were students. He yanked it out of her hands and told me, "Yours, too," and scrutinized these things

like they were foreign currency, not plastic student
IDs attached to W&M lanyards. He asked us if we
were bused in for a program.

This situation is particularly common on campuses in
urban neighborhoods that are either actually high in crime
or (more commonly) understood by the parents and students of the university to be threatening, places like the
University of Pennsylvania on Philly's historically black and
working-class west side. "Penn kids (not me!) would smoke
pot on the campus green and other places without getting
arrested," recalled one Penn alumna "There were fraternities known for hard drugs, and they weren't raided. But
black kids would be frisked right off campus."

This patrolling against perceived outsiders can have cata-
strophic consequences. On July 19, 2015, a University of Cin-
cinnati police officer named Ray Tensing noticed a missing
license plate on a car and approached an unarmed black
man named Samuel Dubose who was sitting in the driver's
seat, just a few blocks from campus. Dubose attempted to
drive off, and Officer Tensing shot and killed him. He and
his colleagues gave an official account of what happened
that differed dramatically, prosecutors said, from what
would later appear on the police video.

Okay, you might say: so elite campuses are disorderly in
a way that might make Kelling and Wilson nervous, and
yes, the community norms allow a whole lot of illicit activity
that wouldn't be tolerated in a poor urban neighborhood.

But the kinds of poor urban neighborhoods that police are charged with keeping orderly are also places of exceedingly high violence. Brown University, for example, lacks shootouts and drive-bys. So, you might argue, police at Brown can tolerate higher levels of disorder.

This is true. I don't want to overcompare what happens on elite campuses and what happens in poor neighborhoods. The constant looming threat of gun violence in the latter alters much of how poor communities experience crime and violence, and much of the way they are policed.

But it is simply not the case that campuses are entirely free of violence or that "disorder" in these places can't plausibly be blamed for leading to a lack of safety. First, the world of Greek life can often be the source of tremendous sadism, abuse, cruelty, and physical danger. In her in-depth exposé of Greek culture, Caitlin Flanagan in the *Atlantic* documents the number of deaths and liability claims associated with Greek houses across the country. "The number of lawsuits that involve paddling gone wrong, or branding that necessitated skin grafts," she writes, "or a particular variety of sexual torture reserved for hazing and best not described in the gentle pages of this magazine, is astounding."

Then there are the shockingly high rates of sexual assault on college campuses. Our best studies indicate that about 20 percent of women are sexually assaulted during their four years on campus. The overwhelming majority of these assaults are committed by someone the survivor knows, and a relatively small group of repeat offenders seem to account for a large portion of the assaults. And only a tiny percentage of these assaults (around 12 percent according to one study) are actually reported.

In 1986 a freshman named Jeanne Clery at Lehigh University in Pennsylvania was raped and murdered in her dorm by a fellow student. Her parents, frustrated with the lack of information from schools about safety on campus, set about advocating for campus safety and successfully lobbied Congress to pass the Clery Act into law in 1990.

The Clery Act compels colleges and universities to report crime on campus to the federal government annually as well as issue warnings to students. Major institutions, from Penn State to Virginia Polytechnic, have been investigated for apparent failures of transparency under the law. Subsequent amendments to the act, and developments in federal guidance on compliance with Title IX of the Civil Rights Act, have required increased reporting of how colleges deal with allegations in their internal disciplinary procedures. In the last several years, thanks to sustained investigative reporting and high-profile cases of systematic mishandling of sexual assault claims (like at Baylor University, which brought down former president and chancellor Kenneth Starr), the issue of sexual assault on campus has once again captured the public's attention.

Michelle Anderson, the president of Brooklyn College, has written extensively on campus justice and sexual assault. She says it's a mistake to view campus rape as a problem distinct from rape more broadly. Given the way rape is dealt with in other environments, from the military chain of command to the regular criminal justice system, she says, it's hard to make a case that the mishandling of the crime on campus is particularly egregious. It's more that the crime of rape itself, she argues, so rooted in conceptions of women as property, has not caught up to our current conception of consent, agency, and violence.

But when the outside world looks at the world of campus justice, it can at first seem downright bizarre that almost none of what happens on campus is ever referred to a judicial system outside the college. Crimes as bad as rape are punished with only a maximum of expulsion, and even that is fairly rare. Over the years, an entirely separate justice system has developed in colleges and universities that encompasses transgressions that are violations of criminal law (theft, rape) and those that aren't (cheating).

It's not just campuses that run their own internal and parallel justice systems. Michelle Anderson, who's also worked with the Department of Defense in developing policies for sexual assault, told me "in the military community, you have exactly the same thing: 'These are our boys. . . . He's a good one. He's one of us. He's a leader in the squadron.' . . . The desire to have a community police itself creates the same kinds of conflicts."

Police departments too have means of internal policing. Most have internal affairs departments, and many cities maintain a putatively independent review authority to look into police misconduct. In Chicago, to take just one example, the Independent Police Review Authority (IPRA) is tasked with investigating complaints and police-involved shootings. Its record speaks for itself: in the period between 2011 and 2015, IPRA received more than 28,500 citizen complaints against police. In 97 percent of the cases, the officers received no punishment. Over the past two years, I've spoken to two separate whistleblowers, both former Chicago cops, who say they were pressured by higher-ups to dismiss cases of what they felt were clear wrongdoing.

This same institutional posture disgraced the Catholic Church during the decades-long child rape scandal. The church had its own canon law, which was, let's say, remarkably forgiving. Priests who clearly were incorrigible threats to child safety were sent for rehabilitation time and time again, shielded from criminal investigation, and given one more shot at redemption, another chance to change their ways, while the numbers of victims mounted.

For all these reasons, we view the notion of an institution "policing itself" with great suspicion. And indeed, the increased attention to campus sexual assault has led to ever-louder calls for these cases to be taken out of the college disciplinary process and placed in the regular criminal justice system. So it is striking that most survivors' advocates I've spoken with oppose the idea—precisely because it would remove the community from policing its own standards and norms. "What I want to do," says Anderson,

> is really help us to see the way that sexism and dismissal of the importance of victimization . . . infects

the criminal justice system, *and* see the way that overreaction in the criminal justice system cannot be the model. Calls for mandatory minimums in the campus context are misguided . . . because of what it means for the ways we think about the possibilities of redemption for all humans. It doesn't mean people don't do bad things. It means people do bad things and can change and can become better.

In 2016 a particularly horrifying campus rape made its way through the regular criminal justice system and, against the odds, actually resulted in a trial and conviction. Brock Turner was a Stanford University freshman and swim team standout. In 2015 two foreign exchange students saw him assaulting a young woman behind a dumpster. He took off running when they spotted him, but the exchange students caught him. He was arrested and eventually convicted.

But Judge Aaron Persky, citing Turner's exemplary record and the "severe impact" it would have on his future, sentenced Turner to six months, despite Turner's apparent lack of remorse, or even real understanding, of what he had done. And so his victim delivered an extraordinary, withering, soulful, and courageous statement that when posted on the Internet quickly racked up millions of views and sparked a national conversation. One cable news host devoted her entire hour on air to reading it.

The broad social rage that the case aroused was exhilarating and righteous but also, somehow, in some way I couldn't quite place at the time, unnerving. When a rich white rapist at an elite school gets only six months in prison, we want the book thrown at him. We want him to get twenty years. And when the judge bends over backward to laud the boy's bright future and talent, ignoring the victim, and when the rapist refuses to take responsibility for the horrible violence and pain he inflicted, we want vengeance. We want the judge punished. We sign petitions calling for him to be recalled. (Indeed, as I write this, an effort to recall Persky from the bench is going ahead full steam.) We want to circulate the rapist's scruffy, glassy-eyed mugshot enough that it replaces the composed image of the swim champ, so that the rapist will know the humiliation of the common criminal.

THE THIRST FOR JUSTICE is undeniably warranted, as when a police officer shoots and kills an unarmed civilian. There should be consequences, there should be a call to account. In some cases, there should be punishment. And these cases serve to highlight the shocking difference between the mechanisms of justice in the Colony and in the Nation. For if anyone gets the full procedural protections of the Nation, of the Fourth and Fifth Amendments, it is the police. In places like Maryland, they enjoy extra statutory protections enshrined in the law called the Law Enforcement Bill of Rights.

But I can't help but feel that in the aftermath of one horrible case after another, we who seek justice are asking the

system to produce a result it will never deliver. The day the
Turner case was making headlines, I happened to be interviewing Elizabeth Gaynes. Previously married to a man who
spent over two decades in prison, Gaynes has spent decades
working with the incarcerated and formerly incarcerated at
the Obsorne Association, the largest service provider of its
kind in New York State. Her friends and colleagues, when
considering the Turner sentence and prominent examples
of elite criminal justice more broadly, had a thirst for "equality of desserts," she said. When two Enron executives, who
were married to each other and had kids, got sentenced,
Gaynes pointed out to me, the judge had the two parents
serve their sentences in succession, "so the kids wouldn't be
disrupted." Where, she asked, is that compassion for others
convicted of crimes? "They never think that keeping our
moms home for our kids mattered."

That experience of two-tiered justice, Gaynes told me,
informed the way she and her colleagues reacted to the
story of Turner's light sentence. "A lot of my colleagues had
that reaction: he should get more time. Then we had to look
at each other and say, 'What the fuck are we talking about?'
All we were offering the victim in that case was incarcera
tion for this guy."

That, says Gaynes, is more or less all we really do offer
crime victims. Not healing, or restitution, or accountability—
just punishment for the offender. Because as all we know,
the American justice system is about wrath and punishment. All we can conceive of with the system we have is

maybe, if everything works, to wrench the privileged down into the pit, to lay low the citizens of the Nation and make them crawl beneath the yoke of the Colony. If we are going to so callously capture and warehouse and harass so many of our citizens, justice commands us to ensure that no one is immune. Let everyone be forced to face the scythe.

But exactly what good does retribution do? If every privileged malefactor in the Nation got his or her proper humiliating comeuppance, if every bad cop went to jail, every bankster executive were sentenced, and every sociopathic rich boy sexual predator were locked up, it would do little to revive democracy and liberty in the occupied precincts of our land. "I spent all morning and early afternoon in criminal court in Brooklyn," the prison abolitionist Mariame Kaba wrote in the midst of the uproar over Brock Turner's sentence.

> Sitting in the sterile, antiseptic gray courtroom watching a parade of young Black men on the assembly line (some handcuffed). The guards, the judge, the overwhelming [number] of lawyers all white administering (white) justice. And I come back here to this ongoing nonsense about the *need* to circulate the mugshot of a convicted white rapist. As though that has ANY purchase at all in dismantling the system I witnessed/participated in today.

This instinct to level down—*Circulate the mugshot! Censure the judge! Get tough on crime for privileged white boys!*—rather than level up is a core feature of American justice. We readily accept punitiveness as the given, as the way we as a democratic polity express ourselves. Our temptation is to seek equality through uniform application of the state's punishing power.

Even the application of mercy, in sentencing or parole, James Whitman argues, can be suspect because it requires judges or parole boards to consider the individual circumstances of each person brought before them, to consider the specific conditions of their crime and detention. And who's to say that showing mercy to one won't mean injustice for another? The only true justice can happen in the absence of mercy, where each individual meets the same punishment and the same fate, with no deviation.

If "no mercy" sounds perverse, keep in mind that injustice in sentencing provided at least part of the rationale that animated the call for mandatory minimums, a policy now seen by many, across the political spectrum, as a wholesale disaster. In the 1960s and 1970s, as Naomi Murakawa details in *The First Civil Right: How Liberals Built Prison America,* influential jurists and legal scholars pointed to shocking racial disparities in sentences for perpetrators of very similar crimes. They located the problem not in institutional racism but in the discretion of the judges themselves, who were empowered to give whatever sentence they wanted. Thus began a push in all levels of law to remove that discretion and impose statutory minimums.

Our discussion of policing and criminal justice is rightly focused on race and racial disparity. But the entire system is out of control. The policing of the Colony has breached the levee and flooded the Nation. SWAT teams are called out in caravans of military vehicles to knock down doors and shoot dogs in the heart of white America, too.

White Americans are more likely to be killed by cops than their peers in any other Western democracy. This is particularly true of poor white and working-class white people. In fact, the places with the highest rates of white incarceration are the most punitive states, those in the conservative Deep South. The result? The states of the Old Confederacy have the *least* amount of racial discrepancy in their incarceration rates. The ratio of the incarceration rates for black people to white people in Louisiana is 4 to 1. In Mississippi it's 3 to 1. In Wisconsin it's 12 to 1; in New Jersey 12.2 to 1.

The incarceration rate just for white Americans is still two and a half times the rate of France. Meaning white America, the Nation, the place free of the worst excesses of law and order and occupation, is still putting its citizens under lock and key at more than twice the rate of its continental cohort. In fact, if white America were its own country, it would have the sixteenth-highest incarceration rate in the world. This is the result of the American impulse to level down.

BUT WHAT IF WE saw everyone in the Colony the same as we do the bright-eyed future swimming star? What if we were to agree human beings are not defined by the worst thing they ever did? Yes, there are incorrigibles and sociopaths. There are pathologically dangerous people who are a threat to those around them, no matter what you try to do to rehabilitate them. But there are far, far fewer of them than are currently crammed twelve to a room in our prisons.

As a full-scale epidemic of opioid addiction has spread through white America, some of the most punitive rhetoric, the staple of how politicians talk about crime, has started to unravel. The images of addicts as dangerous incorrigibles are being replaced by images of high school prom queens lost to the demon of heroin. The shift is striking; the new language of forgiveness is the direct opposite of how Americans reacted to the spike in crack cocaine use among largely inner-city black populations in the late 1980s.

"In Heroin Crisis, White Families Seek Gentler War on Drugs," the *New York Times* reported:

> While heroin use has climbed among all demographic groups, it has skyrocketed among whites. . . . And the growing army of families of those lost to heroin— many of them in the suburbs and small towns—are now using their influence, anger and grief to cushion the country's approach to drugs, from altering the language around addiction to prodding government to treat it not as a crime, but as a disease.

Politicians running for president during the long primary season held town hall after town hall where they counseled family members of addicts, spoke with compassion about the addicts in their own family, and called for treatment, funding, and understanding. This was particularly striking on the Republican side of things, a party more strongly associated with get-tough-on-crime rhetoric.

New Jersey governor Chris Christie, a former federal prosecutor, became something of a viral sensation for his impassioned calls for empathy in the face of suffering. He would discuss his mother's own smoking habit on the trail, saying that when she got sick with lung cancer "no one came to me and said, 'Don't treat her 'cause she got what she deserved.'" Christie would also often speak of a friend who died of an overdose. "There but for the grace of God, go I," he said. "It can happen to anyone. And so we need to start treating people in this country and not jailing them. We need to give them the tools they need to recover. Because every life is precious. *Every* life is an individual gift from God. We have to stop judging, and give them the tools they need to get better."

Stop judging, and give them the tools they need to get better. Think of any other context where this is the guiding ethos of our crime policy.

Imagine a person commits a crime, perhaps even a violent crime, against you. Is this person a human being? A neighbor, a fellow citizen? What do we as a society owe that person? Could he be someone you know and love in the throes of addiction? Or is he a member of a group you'll never encounter again? What dignity is due the perpetrator and the potential perpetrator? Do you and the perpetrator belong to the same country? This is the question before us. The question we've answered wrongly for too long.

Right now the person I conceive as my possible assailant does not inhabit the same Nation as I do. He is in the Colony, and our entire project for decades has been to keep him there. Subtly but unmistakably we have moved the object of our concern from crime to criminals, from acts to essences. It is the criminal, the bad guy, the irredeemable thug, around whom we craft our policy. We must keep him at bay. He is not a man who committed a bad act. He is not a full soul who did something horrible. He is the crime. He is a criminal. He is a subject of the Colony. Citizens can be full human beings; citizens can get second chances; citizens can be forgiven. Subjects are unforgivable.

In Ferguson on the third night of protests, I was out in the streets, broadcasting live. We'd rented a fenced-in parking lot to stage our show, on West Florissant Avenue, where protesters had been met by police with tear gas night after night. A few hundred yards away from where I was broadcasting, a tense standoff was developing between cops and protesters. As they had numerous times, the two sides stood staring at each other. Demonstrators chanted slogans and hurled occasional verbal invective. Cops in riot gear did their best to appear menacing. And then, as usually happened, someone chucked a plastic bottle filled with water, or maybe a rock, and then, *boom!* Out came the tear gas.

If you've never been teargassed, let me say it's a truly vile experience. It feels aggressive. It makes you furious (or I should say, it made me furious). It makes you feel like the cops are there to fight you, and it makes you want to fight them back.

The gas chased the demonstrators down the block past our live location, and as I continued to broadcast, I could hear a bunch of protesters, mostly young people, running down the block, howling with anger and adrenaline. As I faced into the camera, with my back to them, a few of them saw me under the klieg lights, talking into a microphone along with my colleague Craig Melvin. They started chucking rocks.

"Hey, hey, hey." Craig said sternly. He swatted a few away that were headed toward me. "Watch out, Chris."

"*Tell the true story!*" a young woman yelled.

A young man with his face covered walked up and put his hands on the fence. "It ain't just about Mike Brown no more. It's about all people."

I'm standing on one side of the fence, and he's on the other. When we originally scouted the location, we liked the fence in part because it gave us some protection from the police, who the night before had fired a tear gas canister at an Al Jazeera film crew. But now the situation is reversed. Here I am, protected and privileged. And there he is on the other side of the fence. I'm gonna leave Ferguson in a few days, and he's gonna be here with these same cops who just teargassed him.

He moved on. Another young man approached the fence. "You see how they do us out here? They treat us like animals."

Are we part of the same political entity, he and I?

Do we live in the same country?

I'll never see him again. I'll never get pulled over by the Ferguson cops for failing to signal. I'll never be stopped and frisked by the New York City police. Life is pretty damn good in the part of the Nation I live in. It's quiet and peaceful. It's prosperous, and it's *orderly*.

So what would it mean if the Nation and the Colony were joined, if the borders erased, and the humanity—the full, outrageous, maddening humanity—of every single human citizen were recognized and embodied in our society? Or even just to start, in our policing?

I want to think it would be nothing but a net benefit for all. For so long one of the great tools of white supremacy has been to tell white people that there's a fixed pie, and whatever black people get, they lose. As a matter of first principles, I reject that. But it's not just faith that leads me to that belief. In fact, I think all available evidence suggests that the immiseration of large swaths of black and brown America has a negative net effect on white people. A country that, for instance, radically reduced incarceration and increased investment in the human potential of millions of black and brown people would be a richer one. And we know from study after study that racial integration improves measurable outcomes for everyone involved. Integrated schools (which we have largely abandoned) produce net benefits for *all* children, black and white. White people do not need to experience genuine democracy, equality, full citizenship, and recognition for all as a loss or redistribution—eating less so that others may eat more. We can all feast together.

That's my belief as a political matter, and it's what the data show. And yet that's not the whole story. Colonial territories do confer material benefits on their colonizers. That is the entire point of conquest and occupation. Sometimes those benefits are opaque, and in the case of the Colony and the Nation they can be all but illegible. But in Ferguson they were clear; 12 percent of the municipal revenue was raised through tickets. That money was coming disproportionately from the town's black citizens, which meant white people were able to pay lower taxes and make up the difference through harassment of people who didn't look like them.

It's not just Ferguson. In rural economies from upstate New York to downstate Illinois and across the land, in places where all the other employers have left, prisons have become a central source of employment and economic stimulus. On the West Texas plains, in the Mississippi Delta, and in the coalfields of southern Appalachia, the endless stream of prisoners sent to them from the Colony provides livelihoods for the locals. Without them, there would be no work.

Same goes for the $5 billion private prison industry, which is not, in any statistical sense, the cause of the explosion in incarceration but has managed to reap an enormous stream of revenue from it. Once again we see a net transfer of wealth disproportionately from people of color and subjects of the Colony to inhabitants of the Nation who represent the employees, management, and shareholders of these companies.

The Colony pays tribute to the Nation. The citizens enjoy tangible gains *at the expense* of the subjects, even though, or especially when, those gains aren't material. While in some clear cases quantifiable dollars move from one realm to the other, a certain psychological expropriation, a net transfer of well-being, is far more common and far more insidious.

TO BE HONEST, SOME part of me, deep down in my gut, is skeptical that we can radically change policing and justice and society and not have it change my life, too. Some part of me believes, not intellectually but in my skin, that I'm going to have to give something up. Maybe I'll have to give a lot up. Maybe the size of the pie *is* fixed. Maybe equality will cost me something. If it's something material, I don't mind. I can pay higher taxes, if that's what it takes. But that's not what I mean. Maybe true equality would fundamentally alter my way of life, my lived experience of the world in every waking moment.

I remember the bad old days of New York, and I still feel uneasy in places where there are broken windows and vagrants. Maybe everybody does, or maybe just privileged white people do. But if there's one thing I've come to believe, it is that much of the cause of our current state of affairs lies in our tasking police with preserving order rather than with ensuring safety. Order is a slippery thing: it's in the eyes of the beholder and the judgments of the powerful. Safety is clearer: it's freedom from violence and intrusion.

If we abandoned our obsession with order, what would happen? Maybe that stalking unease I felt as a teenager in this city would return. Maybe I'd have to pay a mental tax and reorient my way of thinking, to see sidewalk hustlers and squeegee men not as threats but as part of the social fabric of a community I share. As part of a Nation that is mine but, crucially, *not mine alone.*

IMAGINE A BUTTON THAT would deliver you fifty dollars every time you pressed it. The only catch is that when you pressed the button, someone else, somewhere in the world, would be briefly shocked. There'd be no permanent injuries. You'd never see their faces.

I imagine we'd all agree that it's morally indefensible to push the button. I mean, sure, you might rationalize that in a global sense, your actual happiness gain of fifty dollars would be larger than the other person's temporary discomfort of a shock. And if the person sitting by the button is poor and desperate, I doubt we'd judge her if she pushed the button to feed her kids or get money toward much-needed medicine. But overall it's not okay, as a general principle, to impose random harm on someone else so that you can reap a reward. That's our moral commitment.

Now imagine for a moment this was an actual option—not a test of moral commitment but something people could do. How many would do it? Imagine a frenzied crowd watching people one after another push the button and make their fifty dollars, then line up to do it again. Or imagine the button is in a private booth, hidden from prying eyes and social sanction, like the places where we fill out our ballots.

The temptation to push would be overwhelming. After all, the gain is so tangible and so immediate, so easy to conjure, and the harm so abstract. Someone, somewhere in the world is going to be hurt. Someone you'll never meet and never know.

Now imagine the same button, but rather than dispensing money, pushing it gives you an all-encompassing feeling of security, the warm sense of being rooted and safe. And somewhere, someone you don't know, will experience the opposite, a brief stab of anxiety, the wave of panic and fear.

Again, we know it's wrong, but what if this button is on your smartphone, always there lurking? You could press it whenever you needed that feeling, knowing full well someone else would pay the price. It's tempting to want to feel safe and rooted. It's tempting to want order and comfort, especially if it is delivered free or the cost is paid out of view. But you would never press that button if it made your kids shriek in panic, or if it sent a friend or loved one into a paralyzing spiral of fear. You wouldn't press it if you had to see the results.

The voters who've endorsed the Colony's construction

were selecting from a menu of options. And that menu was put together by shrewd politicians who offered up options that they felt would benefit them and/or neatly play to the white fear that is one of the most singularly explosive forces (if not *the* most explosive force) in American politics.

Our politics has constructed a series of rationales for us to press the button, telling us it's okay to want to press it. *Press the button. Elect me, and you can press it all you want. Elect me, and you'll feel safe.*

If we are going to change this, if our subjects are to truly and finally become our fellow citizens, then we have to stop pressing it.

ON A LOVELY SPRING day about a year ago, as I was beginning to conceive of this book, I was walking alone through Prospect Park. New York City is "diverse," of course, but it's also segregated as hell. The density of the city just means that all the lines are more finely drawn. Block by block, building by building, intersecting and overlapping pockets and niches of Nation and Colony fit together like dovetail joints on a finely crafted piece of wooden furniture.

But Prospect Park is enjoyed by people from both the Colony and the Nation, a borderland between the affluent, predominantly white neighborhoods on the west side (where I live), and the working- and middle-class, predominantly black neighborhoods on the east side.

It is a piece of urban paradise, designed by Frederick Law Olmsted and Calvert B. Vaux, who believed it to be their masterpiece, even greater than Central Park. It has trees, brooks, waterfalls, ponds, long lovely lawns, a lagoon, and endless spaces for residents of the city to grill and play catch and bang drums. On a nice day, the park feels like one of the most exuberant places on earth.

Walking through the park, I saw four black boys on bikes laughing loudly, wildly. I recognized their bearing from my own youth. They were on the edge of puberty, surging with testosterone and mischief, away from any adult supervision, goading each other on. They yelled and menaced passersby. One pretended he was going to run over a man pushing a stroller, then swerved around. When the man said something, he stopped and dismounted his bike. "What'd you say?" he said, his chest out.

The man, there with his infant child, a preschooler, and his wife, shrank away.

Emboldened, the boys pedaled off, swerving and yelling and drawing increasingly concerned and panicked stares from the people (mostly white) walking past. I kept walking, shaking my head, half remembering my own youthful hijinks and half concerned.

A few minutes later I saw them again. They were now even more energized, manic in the way only teenage boys can be. They were shouting at passersby, cussing, stopping to flex and menace.

The one who seemed to be the ringleader then biked up

past a white man who was holding his phone, snatched it out of his hands, and biked off. The man yelled and chased after him and was joined by a few others also yelling. "He took that guy's phone!"

The boys had crossed over from disorderliness to unlawfulness, I thought to myself. Acting the fool was one thing, but taking someone's phone was quite another. Who knew what they would get up to next? I reached for my own phone.

This was the spring of 2015, less than a year since Michael Brown's death and shortly after the unrest in Baltimore. I'd spent months talking to people about police and policing and harassment. I'd watched video after video of police shooting and killing black men and boys. Oftentimes they had been summoned to the scene only because they answered a 911 call about some disturbance—for instance, twelve-year-old Tamir Rice in a Cleveland city park with a pellet gun. I'm sure whoever made that call to the Cleveland police thought they were doing the responsible thing. They thought they were protecting people in that park from harm. But that person pushed a domino that ended that boy's life.

The people in the park continued to shout and chase. The boys on their bikes were pedaling with all their might across a long green lawn.

I took my phone out, held it in my hand, and considered whether to press the button.

AFTERWORD

WHAT WE TALK ABOUT WHEN WE TALK ABOUT CRIME

Though this book was written against the backdrop of Donald Trump's political ascendancy and is, in almost every way, about the forces that carried him to power, it only mentions his name once. I intentionally resisted the temptation to integrate him into this book's arguments, because I wanted to make very clear that the impulses and pathologies I was identifying are much larger than this one man.

And yet here we are.

The first year of the Trump presidency was a disaster in nearly all respects, but it did contain one important silver lining: the unmasking of so much doublespeak in our political vocabulary. As vile as the president's conduct and rhetoric often are, he is also often bracingly forthright about what is normally hidden. For instance, he will say of a candidate he's endorsing or a federal appointee that the person is "loyal" or a "big supporter." Of course that's often a driving concern for politicians, but most at least nod toward a substantive case. Trump just comes out and states the subtext. When asked about his much-criticized appointment of GOP congressman Tom Marino to the position of White House drug czar, Trump's first answer was "Well, he was a very early supporter of mine, the great state of Pennsylvania."

Not: he's got a great record on this issue. Not: he's the perfect man for the job. Not: an affirmative defense of Marino's controversial role in helping to protect Big Pharma as it sold millions of opioid pills (something which would ultimately cause Marino to withdraw his nomination). But rather: he backed me early.

The president is always saying the quiet part loud.

ON THE MORNING OF October 26, 2017, the president took to Twitter (as he so often does at the start of his workday) to endorse Ed Gillespie, Republican candidate for governor in Virginia.

In the ever-evolving "civil war" within the Republican Party, between the establishment and its opponents, Gillespie was as establishment as could be. The man literally ran the Republican National Committee, as well as his own DC lobbying firm. So it was something of a surprise to many that his campaign advertising so thoroughly embraced the white grievance politics that form the core of Trump's anti-establishment message.

Gillespie's campaign advertising focused consistently on the Central American gang MS-13. The gang actually started in Los Angeles prisons and, through US deportation, was then exported back to Central America. It is responsible for horrifying violence across Central America and some ghastly incidents in the US as well. According to the Trump administration, there are 10,000 total members in the US, though Gillespie repeatedly claimed, based on very shaky estimates, that there were 2,000 in Fairfax County alone. One Gillespie ad featured an ominous picture of a shirtless group of Latino men. The man in the center has his face entirely covered in tattoos. Beneath the photo, the ad plasters the words "Kill, Rape, Control." The message is not subtle, even by the standards of political ads. It turns out the men in the picture weren't even MS-13 but, instead, members of a rival gang in El Salvador. Of course, precision isn't the point; it's all about the threat.

Gillespie also ran an ad portraying his opponent, Democrat Ralph Northam, as a supporter of pedophiles and child molesters because he expressed pride that the outgoing, Democratic governor, Terry McAuliffe, had taken action to restore voting rights to felons who had completed their sentences. The ad ends in a split screen pairing Northam with a man caught with 1.7 million images and videos of child pornography.

Most revealingly, Gillespie's campaign advertising focused on Confederate statues. In August of 2017, white supremacists rallied in support of a Robert E. Lee statue in Charlottesville. One of their ranks murdered a counter-protester with his car; others beat a black man bloody; and yet another man, an actual KKK grand wizard from Cleveland, fired a gun at a black man from just a few feet away, right in front of the cops, who did nothing.

The violence precipitated a national conversation about Confederate monuments and a renewed push in Virginia and elsewhere to remove them. Gillespie, who eked out his primary win over a right-wing Confederacy fetishist named Corey Stewart (born and raised in Minneapolis), ended up running his own ad in the general election, proudly declaring his support for the statues of the Confederacy. While Northam wanted to take them down, Gillespie warned, "I'm for keeping 'em up."

All of this was too much for some of Gillespie's mainstream Republican associates.

Bruce Bartlett, a now-rogue Republican who once worked as an economist in the Reagan administration, declared, "I will not be able to vote for my old friend Ed Gillespie for governor. His pandering to racists & neo-Confederates is reprehensible." A senior adviser to Republican senator Rand Paul said, "So the last 3 ads by @EdWGillespie are: gangs, people getting their voting rights back, and monuments. The dog whistle is a little loud, Ed." And the *Washington Post* editorial board, generally timid, genteel, and prone to "both-sides" critiques, laid into Gillespie's ad campaign as "poisonous to Virginia and the nation."

But President Trump and his allies recognized in Gillespie's campaign a junior version of his own. Steve Bannon said Gillespie "closed an enthusiasm gap by rallying around the Trump agenda" and that "Trumpism without Trump" can show the way forward. The president himself embraced the core themes of Gillespie's campaign, tweeting out an endorsement that read: "Ed Gillespie will turn the really bad Virginia economy #'s around, and fast. Strong on crime, he might even save our great statues/heritage!"

Who is the "our," exactly? Is it the heritage of the president, who was born and raised in Queens, New York? The heritage of Ed Gillespie, son of Pemberton Township, New Jersey? Is it the heritage of black Virginians?

No, obviously. "Our" means "white people like us," and to be "strong on crime" in this context has nothing to do with Gillespie's actual policies on criminal prosecution and enforcement—which of course have absolutely nothing to do logically or politically with Confederate statue preservation. The point, made explicit here by a man who makes everything explicit, is that Gillespie's being "strong on crime" means he's committed to white people, to their defense against the dark other; and because he is so committed to the cause of white people, he will also fight to preserve monuments to white supremacy that are now under threat. Trump is saying that Gillespie being "strong on crime" is *why* he will be able to save "our great statues/heritage." In the same way, you might say of a young musical talent, "A gifted singer, she might even make it to Broadway someday."

This wasn't the first time Trump mentioned "crime" in his political endorsements or attacks. When he was trying to boost incumbent Alabama senator Luther Strange against his primary rival Roy Moore, Trump tweeted that Strange was "Strong on Wall & Crime!" When Arizona senator Jeff Flake published a book attacking Trump, the president responded by tweeting that Flake was "WEAK on borders, crime." Of course, if asked, the president would struggle to come up with a single thing to say about Flake's or Strange's actual views or voting record on crime. But crime, as a lived phenomenon, was not what the president was talking about.

WHAT DO WE TALK about when we talk about crime? One of the central arguments of this book is that our discourse around crime is often really a discourse about race, about tribe, about us and them. That when politicians talk about crime and law and order, they are not making policy arguments about how best to preserve public safety, but rather conjuring an image of the world that is a ceaseless battle between Our People (White People) and Those Who Would Seek to Take What's Ours (immigrant gangs, black criminals, various dark marauders). That the language of crime is really the language of white fear, which is an engine of American politics, a propulsive force constantly seeking an outlet.

That's not to say there isn't actual crime: real violence, real trauma, and real threats. MS-13, for example, is a genuinely monstrous organization and has been behind a number of disgusting, violent crimes. In the past two years, there's been a troubling increase in violent crime, particularly homicides in many of America's largest cities. Poor black and brown neighborhoods from Chicago to Cleveland to Baltimore find themselves in the midst of a deepening crisis of violence and despair. These are actual problems that require actual solutions, but for decades politicians have pulled off a kind of bait and switch in which they claim, sometimes plausibly, to be addressing real problems of public safety while essentially manipulating the power of the state to preserve distinct legal and social regimes between the Colony and the Nation. In this way, a spate of shootings in Chicago can be used to drive up fear in Oakland County, Michigan, and a terror attack in New York City can send waves of panic through cable-news viewers in Kansas.

More maddening still, the "strong on crime" rhetoric cloaks itself in plausible deniability. "How dare you call us racists when we're really just concerned about making sure people don't get shot?"

The president, however, barely hides his own bad faith: The cynicism is out in the open. Drawing on ample precedent throughout American history, he's also exported this particular rhetorical device into the question of immigration, shamelessly conflating foreign-born residents with criminality, despite the fact that most studies show immigrants (authorized and unauthorized) commit crimes at lower rates than native-born Americans. One of his very first utterances as a candidate, moments after he came down the gilded escalator, was to declare that Mexico wasn't sending its best to the US. "They're sending people that have lots of problems, and they're bringing those problems with us. They're bringing drugs. They're bringing crime. They're rapists. And some, I assume, are good people."

At the Republican Convention, family members of people who'd been killed by unauthorized immigrants took the podium, while later in office the president signed an executive order that required the Department of Homeland Security to publish a weekly tally of crimes committed by immigrants. Critics noted that Trump's order was literally out of the Nazi playbook; Hitler's press outlets published a weekly digest of crimes committed by Jews.

In cueing voters to associate immigration with criminality, white fear can be set to work its hypnotic magic on immigration the way it has on the "inner city." Having primed their constituents to fear the denizens of the Colony, politicians sold white people on ever more punitive policies as a means of erecting a barrier that would keep out the hordes. Trump offers his base a literal wall between Mexico and the US. The metaphor made reality.

To the president and his political movement, crime is not a problem to be solved. It is a weapon to be wielded.

But truly nothing lays bare the bankruptcy of "law and order" rhetoric like the lawless actions of an administration

that so insistently invokes the term. The Trump administration, which promised its supporters a return to law and
order, has, as of this writing (and surely things will change
by the time you read this), seen its former campaign manager and his deputy indicted for money laundering and
conspiracy against the US. Another staffer pleaded guilty to
lying to federal officials, and at the very moment I write this,
there are reports that the president's former top national
security adviser on the campaign and short-lived head of the
National Security Council is headed for indictment as well.

Remarkably, the president has mustered no outrage
about the alleged crimes of his former staffers. He issued
no righteous condemnation. Quite the opposite: he has
attacked and degraded the FBI and federal law enforcement
whenever it threatens to enforce the law against people
associated with him. Interspersed with these insults are
cries for ruthless enforcement of laws other people break.
In his mind, the system is both persecuting him and too
lenient. Political enemies receive from him no mercy. He
openly directs his own Justice Department to open criminal
investigations of his chief political rival. But when it's his
buddy and associate, he pulls the director of the FBI into a
one-on-one conversation to try to get him to drop his investigation, and then fires him when he doesn't. Trump has
embraced the strongman's philosophy, attributed to Peru-
vian president Óscar Benavides: "For my friends everything,
for my enemies the law."

None of this coheres as a theory of the law. Indeed, the

politician of our time to lean most heavily on the rhetoric of law and order is also the one who cares least about the law. And that's because "law and order" has nothing to do with law, as I argue in the book, and everything to do with order. After all, the president who most famously used the term, the man whose speech gives this book its title, was Nixon himself, a man whose ardor for the law was equally selective.

Despite Nixon's political demise, his success taught us that the enduring power of white fear transcends any one individual who wields it, no matter what ultimate justice they might individually face. Nixon had to shuffle off in disgrace, but the War on Drugs escalated, the rhetoric of law and order intensified, and the prison-industrial complex grew.

And so it will be with Trump, whatever political fate he ultimately meets—one which might befall him before this book makes its way to your hands. Trump is a symptom as much as a cause. His appeal works because it channels the elemental force of American politics. Getting rid of him will be far easier than purging the Nation of the scourge of white fear.

But as impossible as it may seem to imagine some final victory over white fear, it is still a project that we, as citizens, are compelled to pursue.

On Election Day 2017, Democrats in Virginia held their breath. The last two weeks of the campaign had been brutal for their candidate Ed Northam as he appeared to waver on immigration policy; and Gillespie, backed by his white grievance ads, narrowed the polling gap to what looked, on

Election Day, like a near dead heat. The dog whistle may have been loud, it may have been uncouth to some, but it appeared to be working.

Then the returns came back, much earlier than expected, and Northam romped, beating Gillespie by a whopping nine points. Democrats shocked just about every political observer by taking at least 14 House delegate seats with a diverse set of candidates, nearly all of whom defeated conservative white men. Suddenly Gillespie's all-in bet on white grievance looked like a terrible miscalculation.

White fear is a potent force in American politics, but it is not unconquerable. Citizens like you and me collectively determine how much power it has: the fault lies not in our stars but in ourselves. Our collective fate rests in our hands. The borders between the Colony and the Nation are ours to redraw or, should we be audacious enough, annihilate altogether.

Chris Hayes
New York, NY
November 14, 2017

ACKNOWLEDGMENTS

First, I want to thank the many people who took the time to talk to me for this book in cities around the country. Fifteen years into a career as a reporter, I'm still awestruck at the sheer patience and grace people are willing to extend when you ask them to share their experiences.

I was lucky and/or smart enough to hire a phenomenal research assistant in George Aumoithe, whose diligence, brilliance, and razor-sharp critical faculties improved the book immeasurably. (And thanks to Eric Foner for putting me in touch with George.)

A number of folks were kind enough to talk to me while working on the book and offer guidance, expertise, and feedback: Akhil Amar, Peter Moskos, Harold Pollack, John Pfaff, Jelani Cobb, Barry Friedman, Ta-Nehisi Coates, Michelle Anderson, Collier Meyerson, Cassie Fennell, Issa Kohler-Hausmann, Julily Kohler, and Marty Lafalce. Obviously, all the errors that still made it in are mine and mine alone.

This book also could not have happened without the support of everyone at MSNBC, particularly *All In* staffers Allison Koch, Joelle Martinez, Tina Cone, Todd Cole, Brian Montopoli, and Diane Shamis, who all contributed reporting that made its way into the book. They and the entire *All In* team are the best in the business and make me smarter and sharper every day. Denis Horgan, our executive producer, has kept the show steady and thriving even when I was spending long mornings writing. Kristin Osborne is an indefatigable hustler and has been tireless in promoting the show.

My thanks to everyone at Norton, all of whom have been a joy to work with. Huge thanks to my editor, Tom Mayer, who in a very real sense conceived this book when he sent an email to my agent, Will Lippincott, asking if I'd ever considered writing a book about policing. He's been a rock. Rachel Salzman is incredible at her job. She and the rest of the Norton team—Sarah Bolling, Bill Rusin, Meredith McGinnis, Steve Colca, Don Rifkin, Julia Druskin, Janet Biehl, Elisabeth Kerr, Mary Kate Skehan, and Laura Goldin—have all worked feverishly to make this book a success. I am deeply grateful for their labor. And my relationship with Will Lippincott continues to be one of the most rewarding of my professional life.

Finally, none of this book would've happened without my family. My parents, Roger and Geri, raised me in the Bronx and taught me and my brother to love the city and all it offered, something my wife and I are trying to pass along to our little New Yorkers Ryan and David. (With the help of their uncle Luke.) And at every step in my journey as an adult—from waiting tables to writing and broadcasting—I've relied on my wife Kate as an intellectual, emotional, and spiritual partner. She is hands down the single best editor I have ever met, and she worked her magic on this book, improving it with every single tug and tweak. But more generally, she is everything good in my life. If this book is any good, that's mostly her, too.

NOTES

I

20 **a young man named Freddie Gray:** "Man Critically Hurt in Taped Police Encounter," *Baltimore Sun,* April 14, 2015; Kevin Rector and Jean Marbella, "Injuries in Van Ride Focus of City Probe," *Baltimore Sun,* April 21, 2015; Scott Dance, "Gray Injury Suggests 'Forceful Trauma': Doctors Compare It to Impact from a Car Accident," *Baltimore Sun,* April 21, 2015.

20 **His death triggered:** "Freddie Gray's Funeral, Burial Set for Monday," *Baltimore Sun,* April 25, 2015; Luke Broadwater, "Police Brace for March: Protest Today; Officials Acknowledge Mistakes in Death of Freddie Gray," *Baltimore Sun,* April 25, 2015; Julie Scharper, "A Week After Freddie Gray's Death, Mourners Gather to Pay Respects," *Baltimore Sun,* April 27, 2015; Kevin Rector, Yvonne Wenger, and Jessica Anderson, "Protests Continue: Clashes Contrast with Street Dancing as Police and Troops Seek to Establish Calm," *Baltimore Sun,* April 29, 2015.

20 **bracing for the trials:** Justin Fenton, "Six Baltimore Police Officers Indicted in Death of Freddie Gray," *Baltimore Sun,* May 21, 2015.

20 **None of them would be:** Kevin Rector, "Charges Dropped, Freddie

Gray Case Concludes with Zero Convictions Against Officers," *Baltimore Sun*, July 27, 2016.

20 **"My initial motivation":** Dayvon Love, interviewed on *All In with Chris Hayes*, MSNBC, November 6, 2015.

20 **Today Love coaches:** "Baltimore Students Redefine the Rules of Debate," NPR, April 7, 2008.

22 **the most violent developed country:** Erin Grinshteyn and David Hemenway, "Violent Death Rates: The US Compared with Other High-Income OECD Countries, 2010," *American Journal of Medicine* 129, no. 3 (March 1, 2016): 266–73, doi:10.1016/j.amjmed.2015.10.025.

22 **the most incarcerated:** Michelle Ye Hee Lee, "Yes, U.S. Locks People up at a Higher Rate than Any Other Country," *Washington Post*, July 7, 2015.

22 **the country's homicide rate:** *Crime in the United States 1995*, Uniform Crime Reporting, U.S. Department of Justice, FBI, n.d., https://ucr.fbi.gov/crime-in-the-u.s/1995; *Crime in the United States 2015, January-June*, Uniform Crime Reporting, U.S. Department of Justice, FBI, n.d., https://ucr.fbi.gov/crime-in-the-u.s/2015/preliminary-semiannual-uniform-crime-report-januaryjune-2015; Andy Kiersz and Brett LoGiurato et al., "Obama Was Right When He Said 'This Type of Mass Violence Does Not Happen in Other Developed Countries,'" *Business Insider*, June 18, 2015; *Global Study on Homicide 2013*, UN Office on Drugs and Crime, n.d., https://www.unodc.org/gsh/.

22 **imprisons a higher percentage:** Lisa Mahapatra, "Incarcerated in America: Why Are So Many People in US Prisons? [CHARTS]," *International Business Times*, March 19, 2014.

23 **rivals the number of Russians:** Adam Gopnik, "The Caging of America," *New Yorker*, January 30, 2012; Fareed Zakaria, "Incarceration Nation," *Time*, April 2, 2012; "US Prison Industrial Complex Versus the Stalinist Gulag," *Sean's Russia Blog*, May 11, 2013, http://seansrussiablog.org/2013/05/11/us-prison-industrial-complex-versus-the-stalinist-gulag/.

23   **Nearly one out of every four:** Michelle Ye Hee Lee, "Does the United
     States Really Have 5 Percent of the World's Population and One
     Quarter of the World's Prisoners?," *Washington Post,* April 30, 2015.

23   **Black men aged 20 to 34:** "Collateral Costs: Incarceration's Effect
     on Economic Mobility," Pew Charitable Trusts, September 28, 2010,
     p. 31.

23   **a grand total of three:** *The Right Investment?: Corrections Spending in
     Baltimore City,* Justice Policy Institute and Prison Policy Initiative, Feb-
     ruary 2015, http://www.prisonpolicy.org/origin/md/report.html.

23   **a homicide rate that is 9,000:** "The Debate over Crime Rates Is
     Ignoring the Metric That Matters Most: 'Murder Inequality,'"
     Trace, July 25, 2016, https://www.thetrace.org/2016/07/crime-rates
     -american-cities-murder-inequality/.

24   **a once-in-a-century:** William J. Stuntz, *The Collapse of American Crimi-
     nal Justice* (Cambridge, MA: Belknap Press of Harvard University
     Press, 2011), 254.

24   **The scope of this social upheaval:** Uniform Crime Reporting Sta-
     tistics, Database, U.S. Department of Justice, FBI, n.d., http://www
     .ucrdatatool.gov/.

25   **In 1965 the unrest:** Peter B. Levy, "The Dream Deferred: The Assas-
     sination of Martin Luther King, Jr., and the Holy Week Uprisings of
     1968," in *Baltimore '68: Riots and Rebirth in an American City,* ed. Jes-
     sica Elfenbein, Elizabeth Nix, and Thomas Hollowak (Philadelphia:
     Temple University Press, 2011), Kindle ed., loc. 243.

31   **Stokely Carmichael and Charles V. Hamilton published:** *Black
     Power: The Politics of Liberation in America* (New York: Vintage, 1967).

31   **"nation within a nation.":** Kenneth B. Clark, *Dark Ghetto: Dilemmas of
     Social Power* (Hanover, NH: University Press of New England, 1989).

33   **"Rather than rely on race":** Michelle Alexander, *The New Jim Crow:
     Mass Incarceration in the Age of Colorblindness* (New York: New Press,
     2012), Kindle ed., p. 2, loc. 202.

35   **the semantic trick of racial vocabulary:** Karen E. Fields and Bar-

bara J. Fields, *Racecraft: The Soul of Inequality in American Life* (2012; reprint London: Verso, 2014), Kindle ed., p. 17, loc. 272.

36 **The two-block stretch:** "Nearly half of the city's police calls" went to Section 8 apartments. Jesse Bogan Moskop Walker, "As Low-Income Housing Boomed, Ferguson Pushed Back," *St. Louis Post-Dispatch*, October 19, 2014.

38 **"Do not treat criminals":** *Investigation of the Baltimore City Police Department*, U.S. Department of Justice, Civil Rights Division, August 10, 2016, p. 29.

39 **As of 2008, nearly 15 percent:** Bruce Western and Becky Pettit, "Incarceration & Social Inequality," *Dædalus*, Summer 2010.

II

43 **"They are marching toward us":** Ray Downs, "Police in Ferguson Fire Tear Gas on Protesters Standing in Their Own Backyard," *Riverfront Times* (St. Louis), August 12, 2014, http://www.riverfronttimes .com/newsblog/2014/08/12/police-in-ferguson-fire-tear-gas-on-protesters-standing-in-their-own-backyard; Ray Downs, "Ferguson Police Fire Tear Gas on Protester with 'Hands Up' in Their Own Backyard" (video), *YouTube*, https://www.youtube.com/watch?v=qXhtvd 0o2Fw.

44 **when he was shot:** Western and Pettit, "Incarceration & Social Inequality."

46 **a sixteen-year-old-foster child:** The pupil later faced a charge for disturbing schools, as did Niya Kenny, the classmate who filmed the incident. See Loren Thomas, "Student Arrested Says She Was Standing Up for Classmate," *WLTX* (Columbia, SC), October 28, 2015, http://www.wltx.com/news/local/student-arrested-says-she-was-standing-up-for-classmate/234859036.

47 **"The poorest man may":** William Pitt, speech on the Excise Bill (1763), as quoted in *Miller v. United States*, 357 U.S. 301, 307 (1958).

47 **"The gentleman on the left"**: Brandon Friedman, Twitter post, August 13, 2014, https://twitter.com/bfriedmandc/status/49972873 3830676480?lang=en.

52 **"a set of lawless piratical"**: British Admiral John Montagu, as quoted in Peter Andreas, *Smuggler Nation: How Illicit Trade Made America* (New York: Oxford University Press, 2014), Kindle ed., loc. 422.

53 **Between 1680 and 1682:** Ibid., loc. 352–53.

54 **Between 1710 and 1760:** Ibid., loc. 354.

55 **"While it is true that any"**: *Floyd v. City of New York*, 959 F. Supp. 2d 540, 557 (U.S. District Court for the Southern District of New York, 2013).

56 **"The house of every one"**: I am grateful to Barry Friedman and Akhil Amar for helping me understand this line of cases.

56 **"enable[d] the custom house officers"**: John Adams to William Tudor, Sr., March 29, 1817, National Archives: Founders Online, http://founders.archives.gov/documents/Adams/99-02-02-6735.

58 **"worst instrument of arbitrary power"**: James Otis, "Against Writs of Assistance" (February 24, 1761), Constitution Society, http://www.constitution.org/bor/otis_against_writs.htm.

58 **"Every man of an immense"**: John Adams as quoted in Andreas, *Smuggler Nation*, loc. 617, emphasis added. See also James Farrell, "The Child Independence Is Born: James Otis and Writs of Assistance," *Communication Scholarship*, January 1, 2014, http://scholars.unh.edu/comm_facpub/5.

60 **"Convert the brave, honest officers"**: Benjamin Franklin, as quoted in Andreas, *Smuggler Nation*, loc. 663.

61 **"sent hither swarms of officers"**: Ibid., loc. 803.

62 **"Ferguson's law enforcement practices"**: *Investigation of the Ferguson Police Department*, U.S. Department of Justice, Civil Rights Division, March 4, 2015, p. 2.

63 **disproportionately empowered:** Matt Pearce, "Ferguson Officials,

Now Mostly Black like the City, Still Face Federal Suit over Police Reforms," *Los Angeles Times*, February 25, 2016; Trymaine Lee, "Michael Brown Shooting Unearths Ferguson's Deeper Troubles," MSNBC, August 12, 2014.

64 **"unless ticket writing ramps up":** *Investigation of Ferguson Police Department*, pp. 9–10.

64 **"at disproportionately high rates":** Ibid., p. 5.

65 **"We spoke, for example":** Ibid., p. 4.

67 **"*Lieutenant*: Get over here":** Ibid., pp. 17–18.

67 **arrested and detained journalists:** Mark Berman, "Washington Post Reporter Charged with Trespassing, Interfering with a Police Officer," *Washington Post*, August 10, 2015.

68 **"In the colonies, the official":** Frantz Fanon, *The Wretched of the Earth*, trans. Richard Philcox (New York: Grove Press, 2004), Kindle ed., p. 3, loc. 880.

70 **"In the summer of 2012":** *Investigation of Ferguson Police Department*, 3.

71 **"There is the man at the top":** Frantz Fanon, *Black Skin, White Masks*, trans. Richard Philcox (New York: Grove Press, 2008), Kindle ed., p. 187, loc. 2361.

72 **"In response he was tarred":** Andreas, *Smuggler Nation*, loc. 738.

72 **"put in the stocks":** Carl E. Prince and Mollie Keller, *The U.S. Customs Service: A Bicentennials History* (Washington, D.C.: Department of the Treasury, U.S. Customs Service, 1989), p. 23, http://archive.org/details/uscustomsservice00prin.

72 **"colonialism is not a thinking":** Fanon, *Wretched of the Earth*, p. 23, loc. 1171.

74 **"I-270 traffic enforcement":** *Investigation of Ferguson Police Department*, pp. 13–14.

75 **identical violations:** Radley Balko, "How Municipalities in St. Louis County, Mo., Profit from Poverty," *Washington Post*, September 3, 2014.

III

81   **"Shots fired":** Cleveland 19 Digital Team, "CPD Releases 911, Dispatch Calls and Survcillance Video from Officer-Involved Shooting," *FOX19Now,* November 26, 2014.

82   **"observed a large sign":** *Investigation of Cleveland Division of Police,* U.S. Department of Justice, Civil Rights Division, December 4, 2014, p. 6.

83   **"moves through Harlem":** James Baldwin, "Fifth Avenue, Uptown," *Esquire,* July 1960, reprinted in *Esquire,* October 16, 2007.

84   **"At night, when we were going aboard":** Ed Southern, ed., *The Jamestown Adventure: Accounts of the Virginia Colony, 1605–1614* (Winston-Salem, N.C.: John F. Blair, 2011), Kindle ed., loc. 265.

85   **In 1622, Myles Standish:** Nathaniel Philbrick, *Mayflower: A Story of Courage, Community, and War* (New York: Viking Press, 2006), Kindle ed., loc. 2281; Edward Winslow, "Good Newes from New England" (1624), *Plymouth Colony Archive Project,* http://www.histarch.illinois.cdu/plymouth/goodnews5.html.

85   **"The savagery":** Bernard Bailyn, *The Barbarous Years: The Peopling of British North America: The Conflict of Civilizations, 1600–1675* (New York: Knopf, 2012), Kindle ed., p. 438, loc. 8180.

86   **"The slaves, deaf to all":** James Walvin, *Short History of Slavery* (London: Penguin UK, 2007), Kindle cd., p. 121, loc. 1947.

87   **"plunder":** Ta-Nehisi Coates, "The Case for Reparations," *Atlantic,* June 2014.

89   **"So I'm working last week":** "People, Please Stop Making My Job So Difficult. • /r/ProtectAndServe," *Reddit,* n.d., https://www.reddit.com/r/ProtectAndServe/comments/34zwuw/people_please_stop_making_my_job_so_difficult/.

94   **The typical cadet training:** Brian A. Reaves, "State and Local Law Enforcement Training Academies, 2006," Bureau of Justice Statistics, February 2009, p. 6, http://www.bjs.gov/content/pub/pdf/slleta06.pdf.

96 **"If a mental health unit":** "Police Officer Who Killed Unarmed, Naked Veteran Charged with Murder," *ThinkProgress,* January 22, 2016.

97 **in 2015 a full quarter:** Wesley Lowery et al., "Distraught People, Deadly Results: Fatal Shootings by On-Duty Police Officers," *Washington Post,* June 30, 2015.

102 **more than one gun:** Scott Horsely, "Guns in America, By the Numbers," NPR, January 5, 2016.

103 **two police officers were shot:** "2 Cops Shot Outside Ferguson Police Headquarters," *CBS News,* March 12, 2015.

103 **Japanese police only began:** David B. Kopel, "Japanese Gun Control," Asia Pacific Law Review 2 (1993): 26–52, accessed at GunCite .com, http://www.guncite.com/journals/dkjgc.html, and Chris Weller, "Japan Has Almost Completely Eliminated Gun Deaths— Here's How," Business Insider, November 6, 2017, at http://www .businessinsider.com/gun-control-how-japan-has-almost-completely-eliminated-gun-deaths-2017-10.

104 **"We have a war:** *O.J.: Made in America,* ESPN Films, Laylow Films, 2016.

105 **SWAT teams:** Radley Balko, *Rise of the Warrior Cop: The Militarization of America's Police Forces* (Philadelphia: PublicAffairs/Perseus Books, 2013).

105 **"Under this warrior worldview":** Seth Stoughton, "Law Enforcement's 'Warrior' Problem," *Harvard Law Review,* April 10, 2015.

IV

110 **Between 1960 and 1980:** John F. Pfaff, "Escaping the Standard Story: Why the Conventional Wisdom on Prison Growth Is Wrong, and Where We Can Go from Here," *Fordham Law Legal Studies,* Research Paper no. 2414596 (March 25, 2014): p. 7, http://ssrn.com/ abstract=2414596.

110   **But starting in 1980:** "Punishment Rate Measures Prison Use Rela-
      tive to Crime," Pew Charitable Trusts, March 23, 2016, http://pew
      .org/1RBTAin.

110   **When President Nixon signed:** "The Controlled Substances Act
      (CSA): Overview," *Findlaw*, n.d., http://criminal.findlaw.com/
      criminal-charges/controlled-substances-act-csa-overview.html.

111   **The number of people in state:** "Fact Sheet: Trends in U.S. Cor-
      rections," Sentencing Project, December 2015, p. 3, http://
      sentencingproject.org/wp-content/uploads/2016/01/Trends-in-
      US-Corrections.pdf; Nathan James, "The Federal Prison Population
      Buildup: Options for Congress," Congressional Research Service,
      May 20, 2016, https://www.fas.org/sgp/crs/misc/R42937.pdf.

111   **The Nixon campaign in 1968:** Dan Baum, "Legalize It All," *Harper's
      Magazine*, April 2016.

111   **In 1980 the percentage:** Ryan S. King, "Disparity by Geography: The
      War on Drugs in America's Cities," Sentencing Project, May 2008,
      p. 6, http://www.sentencingproject.org/publications/disparity-by-
      geography-the-war-on-drugs-in-americas-cities/.

112   **black people are four times more likely:** Ian Urbina, "Marijuana
      Arrests Four Times as Likely for Blacks," *New York Times*, June 3,
      2013; *The War on Marijuana in Black and White*, American Civil Lib-
      erties Union, June 2013, 17–21, https://www.aclu.org/feature/war-
      marijuana-black-and-white.

112   **only about 20 percent:** Pfaff, "Escaping the Standard Story," 4.

113   **Before the Sentencing Reform Act of 1984:** William J. Sabol and
      John C. McGready, "Time Served in Prison by Federal Offenders,
      1986-97," Bureau of Justice Statistics, June 1, 1999, http://www.bjs
      .gov/index.cfm?ty=pbdetail&iid=868.

113   **number of arrests for drug law violations:** "Drugs and Crime Facts,"
      Bureau of Justice Statistics, n.d., http://www.bjs.gov/content/dcf/
      enforce.cfm.

113   **number of people being thrown into:** John F. Pfaff, "The Myths

and Realities of Correctional Severity: Evidence from the National Corrections Reporting Program on Sentencing Practices," *American Law and Economics Review* 13, no. 2 (October 1, 2011): 492–96, doi:10.1093/aler/ahr010.

114 **"The criminal justice system is"**: Pfaff, "Escaping the Standard Story," 11.

115 **white people rate children:** Philip Atiba Goff et al., "The Essence of Innocence: Consequences of Dehumanizing Black Children," *Journal of Personality and Social Psychology* 106, no. 4 (2014): 529, 541.

116 **"scared and nervous":** Ikimulisa Livingston, "Sean Bell Cop Was 'Scared and Nervous' Before Shooting," *New York Post,* March 20, 2008.

121 **New York City set a record:** George James, "New York Killings Set a Record, While Other Crimes Fell in 1990," *New York Times,* April 23, 1991.

121 **it had 100,280 robberies:** "CompStat," City of New York Police Department, n.d., http://www.nyc.gov/html/nypd/downloads/pdf/crime_statistics/cs-en-us-city.pdf.

121 **In 1960 there were approximately:** Uniform Crime Reporting Statistics, Database, U.S. Department of Justice, FBI, http://www.ucrdatatool.gov/.

121 **"To be black in the Baltimore":** Ta-Nehisi Coates, *Between the World and Me* (New York: Spiegel & Grau, 2015), Kindle ed., p. 17, loc. 179.

123 **in the Crack Years black citizens:** James Forman, Jr., *Locking Up Our Own: Crime and Punishment in Black America* (New York: Farrar, Straus and Giroux, 2017).

124 **"drug thugs and gun thugs":** Mary Jordan, "Barry Seeks Money Trail from Drugs," *Washington Post,* April 13, 1989.

124 **fight over the 1994 crime bill:** Elizabeth Hinton, Julilly Kohler-Hausmann, and Vesla M. Weaver, "Did Blacks Really Endorse the 1994 Crime Bill?," *New York Times,* April 13, 2016.

125 **"to say Black people":** Mariame Kaba, Twitter post, October 12, 2015, https://twitter.com/prisonculture/status/653637024323387392.

128 **The rate varies by locality:** Martin Kaste, "Open Cases: Why One-Third of Murders in America Go Unresolved," NPR, March 30, 2015.

129 **"Like the schoolyard bully":** Jill Leovy, *Ghettoside: A True Story of Murder in America* (New York: Spiegel & Grau, 2015), Kindle ed., p. 9, loc. 283.

129 **the best predictor of whether:** "Death Penalty Sentencing: Research Indicates Pattern of Racial Disparities," U.S. Government Accountability Office, February 26, 1990, p. 5, http://www.gao.gov/products/GGD-90-57.

131 **definitively false:** Justin Fenton, "Autopsy of Freddie Gray Shows 'High-Energy' Impact," *Baltimore Sun,* June 24, 2015.

132 **"They were coming downtown":** Pete Hamill, "A Savage Disease Called New York," *New York Post,* April 23, 1989.

133 **"today discrimination against whites":** Janell Ross, "White Americans Long for the 1950s, When They Didn't Face So Much Discrimination," *Washington Post,* November 17, 2015.

134 **"including cancer or heart disease":** Gillian K. SteelFisher, Robert J. Blendon, and Narayani Lasala-Blanco, "Ebola in the United States—Public Reactions and Implications," *New England Journal of Medicine* 373, no. 9 (August 27, 2015): 789–91, doi:10.1056/NEJMp 1506290.

134 **killed by their own furniture:** Andrew Shaver, "You're More Likely to Be Fatally Crushed by Furniture than Killed by a Terrorist," *Washington Post,* November 3, 2015.

136 **between 1993 and 2014:** Jennifer L. Truman and Lynn Langton, "Criminal Victimization, 2014," Bureau of Justice Statistics, August 2015, http://www.bjs.gov/content/pub/pdf/cv14.pdf; "Crime," Gallup, n.d., http://www.gallup.com/poll/1603/Crime.aspx.

137 **In 2016 Gallup found:** "In U.S., Concern About Crime Climbs to

15-Year High," Gallup, April 6, 2016, http://www.gallup.com/poll/
190475/americans-concern-crime-climbs-year-high.aspx.

V

144 **great migration of black people:** Isabel Wilkerson, *The Warmth of
Other Suns: The Epic Story of America's Great Migration* (New York: Vintage, 2010).

144 **long-standing de facto segregation:** Martha Biondi, *To Stand and
Fight: The Struggle for Civil Rights in Postwar New York City* (Cambridge,
Mass.: Harvard University Press, 2006).

144 **Federal policy facilitated:** Arnold R. Hirsch, *Making the Second
Ghetto: Race and Housing in Chicago 1940–1960* (Chicago: University
of Chicago Press, 1998); Robert O. Self, *American Babylon: Race and
the Struggle for Postwar Oakland* (Princeton, NJ: Princeton University
Press, 2005); Kenneth T. Jackson, *Crabgrass Frontier: The Suburbanization of the United States* (New York: Oxford University Press, 1985).

145 **Martin Luther King, Jr., marched through Chicago:** David Bern-
stein, "The Longest March," *Chicago*, July 25, 2016.

145 **"You start out in 1954":** Atwater, was, paradoxically, making a case
for why Republican rhetoric was actually *improving*. See Rick Perl-
stein, "Exclusive: Lee Atwater's Infamous 1981 Interview on the
Southern Strategy," *Nation*, November 13, 2012.

146 **Michael Griffith:** Robert D. McFadden, "Black Man Dies After Beating by Whites in Queens," *New York Times*, December 21, 1986.

146 **Yusef Hawkins:** Ralph Blumenthal, "Black Youth Is Killed by
Whites; Brooklyn Attack Is Called Racial," *New York Times*, August
25, 1989.

147 **"From now on the Republicans":** James Boyd, "Nixon's Southern
Strategy 'It's All In the Charts,'" *New York Times*, May 17, 1970.

151 **The footage of Ronald Reagan:** Dorsey Shaw, "Ronald Reagan
Visited the South Bronx in 1980. You Can Probably Imagine What

Happened Next" (video), *YouTube*, https://www.youtube.com/watch?
v=HcoQTPxnIqw.

152 **"They should fix up":** William E. Geist, "Residents Give a Bronx
Cheer to Decal Plan," *New York Times*, November 12, 1983.

153 **"residents of the foot patrolled":** George L. Kelling and James Q.
Wilson, "Broken Windows: The Police and Neighborhood Safety,"
Atlantic, March 1982.

160 **violent crimes in the subways:** Jacques Steinberg, "Subway Crime
Fell in 1991, Officials Say," *New York Times*, February 21, 1992.

161 **"While there is some variance":** Franklin E. Zimring, *The Great
American Crime Decline* (New York: Oxford University Press, 2008),
Kindle ed., loc. 295, 309.

162 **"Misdemeanor justice in New York City":** Issa Kohler-Hausmann,
"Managerial Justice and Mass Misdemeanors," *Stanford Law Review*
66, no. 3 (March 2014).

163 **Between 1991 and 2015:** Patrick McGeehan, "Record Number of
Tourists Visited New York City in 2015, and More Are Expected This
Year," *New York Times*, March 8, 2016.

163 **amount those visitors spent:** "NYC Statistics," Nycgo.com, http://
www.nycgo.com/research/nyc-statistics-page.

163 **application boom:** Karen W. Arenson, "New York Siren Song Lures
More College Applications," *New York Times*, September 9, 1998; Wil-
liam H. Honan, "Applicants Inundate Colleges Great and Modest,"
New York Times, February 17, 1999.

163 **increases in real estate value:** E. B. Solomont, "When Will the
Boom Break?," *Real Deal*, April 1, 2015, http://therealdeal.com/
issues_articles/when-will-the-boom-break/.

164 **"situated on a quiet residential area":** "29 Mount Morris Park W,"
Corcoran Group, Corcoran.com/nyc/Listings/Display/3646665.

166 **capital was so scarce:** "Community Development Corporations
(CDCs)," Community-Wealth, June 21, 2012, http://community-
wealth.org/strategies/panel/cdcs/index.html.

166 **In 1984 poor Americans:** Matthew Desmond, "Unaffordable America: Poverty, Housing, and Eviction," Fast Focus 22 (March 2015), http://www.irp.wisc.edu/publications/fastfocus/pdfs/FF22-2015.pdf.

167 **Due to rising rents:** Matthew Desmond, *Evicted: Poverty and Profit in the American City* (New York: Crown, 2016).

171 **the central, key factor:** Erin Durkin, Sarah Ryley, and Jennifer Fermino, "De Blasio Defends 'Broken Windows' Policing After Daily News Analysis," *New York Daily News*, August 5, 2014.

171 **"Because of that [crime] bill":** Robert Farley, "Bill Clinton and the 1994 Crime Bill," *FactCheck*, April 12, 2016, http://www.factcheck.org/2016/04/bill-clinton-and-the-1994-crime-bill/.

172 **crime dropped across all categories:** Franklin E. Zimring, *The Great American Crime Decline* (New York: Oxford University Press, 2008), Kindle ed., loc. 192.

172 **across all geographic areas:** Ibid., loc. 228.

172 **even property crimes continued:** Christopher Uggen, "Crime and the Great Recession," Stanford Center on Poverty and Inequality and Russell Sage Foundation, October 2012, https://web.stanford.edu/group/recessiontrends/cgi-bin/web/sites/all/themes/barron/pdf/Crime_fact_sheet.pdf

172 **a huge number of men entered:** Dana Goldstein, "10 (Not Entirely Crazy) Theories Explaining the Great Crime Decline," *Marshall Project*, November 24, 2014, https://www.themarshallproject.org/2014/11/24/10-not-entirely-crazy-theories-explaining-the-great-crime-decline.

172 **Mass incarceration also played some role:** Justin Wolfers, David Leonhardt, and Kevin Quealy, "1.5 Million Missing Black Men," *New York Times*, April 20, 2015.

173 **varying levels of environmental lead:** "Sick Kids Are Just the Beginning of America's Lead Crisis," *Mother Jones*, February 11, 2016.

173 **During the Crack Years of the mid-1980s:** Roland Fryer et al., "Mea-

suring Crack Cocaine and Its Impact," *Economic Inquiry* 51, no. 3 (April 2006): 1651–81.

174 **"no support for a simple":** Bernard E. Harcourt and Jens Ludwig, "Broken Windows: New Evidence from New York City and a Five-City Social Experiment," *University of Chicago Law Review* 73, no. 1 (2006): 271–320.

174 **"are associated with an overall":** Anthony A. Braga, Brandon C. Welsh, and Cory Schnell, "Can Policing Disorder Reduce Crime? A Systematic Review and Meta-Analysis," *Journal of Research in Crime and Delinquency* 52, no. 4 (July 1, 2015): 567–88, doi:10.1177/0022427815576576.

176 **essentially zero relationship:** Emily Badger, "12 Years of Data from New York City Suggest Stop-and-Frisk Wasn't That Effective," *Washington Post*, August 21, 2014.

176 **"Ferguson effect":** Christine Byers, "Crime Up After Ferguson and More Police Needed, Top St. Louis Area Chiefs Say," *St. Louis Post-Dispatch*, November 15, 2014.

177 **"new national crime wave":** Heather Mac Donald, "The New Nationwide Crime Wave," *Wall Street Journal*, May 29, 2015.

177 **"fetal" position:** Derrick Blakley, "Emanuel: Fear of Being Recorded May Be Discouraging Cops from Doing Their Jobs," *CBS Chicago*, October 12, 2015.

177 **a historic low:** Ashley Southall, "Decline in Stop-and-Frisk Tactic Drives Drop in Police Actions in New York, Study Says," *New York Times*, December 11, 2015.

VI

182 **those electorates often draw:** William J. Stuntz, *The Collapse of American Criminal Justice*, (Cambridge, Mass.: Belknap Press of Harvard University Press, 2011), Kindle ed., locs. 3281, 337, 363.

183 **why the U.S. criminal justice system compares:** James Q. Whit-

man, *Harsh Justice: Criminal Punishment and the Widening Divide Between America and Europe* (New York: Oxford University Press, 2005), Kindle ed., loc. 90–93.

183 **punishment as a great equalizer:** Ibid., loc. 39.

184 **"Over the course of the last":** Ibid., loc. 131.

184 **"Where nineteenth-century continental":** Ibid., loc. 150.

185 **almost all crime in the United States:** Amy Sherman, "The Actual Statistics About Black-on-Black Murders," *PolitiFact Florida*, May 21, 2015.

186 **"We ask that you treat [Horton's] case":** Beth Schwartzapfel and Bill Keller, "Willie Horton Revisited," *Marshall Project*, May 13, 2015, https://www.themarshallproject.org/2015/05/13/willie-horton-revisited.

186 **every single U.S. state:** Martin Tolchin, "Study Says 53,000 Got Prison Furloughs in '87, and Few Did Harm," *New York Times*, October 12, 1988.

186 **"More than 20,000 already have":** Doug Willis, "Gov. Reagan Also Had Problems with Prison Work Furlough Program," *Associated Press*, June 26, 1988.

188 **"licensed as RI Special Police Officers":** "About the Department," Brown University Department of Public Safety, https://www.brown.edu/about/administration/public-safety/about-department.

195 **"decent folk":** Kelling and Wilson, "Broken Windows."

198 **Ray Tensing:** The case against Ray Tensing ended in a mistrial on November 12, 2016. Just before this book went to press, the Hamilton County prosecuting attorney announced that he would seek to retry the case against the former officer.

199 **"The number of lawsuits that involve":** Caitlin Flanagan, "The Dark Power of Fraternities," *Atlantic*, March 2014.

199 **about 20 percent of women:** Kelly Wallace, "Study: Nearly 20 Percent of College Freshmen Victims of Rape," CNN, May 20, 2015; Jeff Nesbit, "Incapacitated Rape Is a Big Problem," *US News & World Report*, November 18, 2015.

199 **someone the survivor knows:** "National Intimate Partner and Sexual Violence Survey," Centers for Disease Control and Prevention, n.d., http://www.cdc.gov/violenceprevention/pdf/nisvs_factsheet-a.pdf.

200 **only a tiny percentage:** Sofi Sinozich and Lynn Langton, "Rape and Sexual Assault Victimization Among College-Age Females, 1995–2013," Bureau of Justice Statistics, December 2014, http://www.bjs.gov/content/pub/pdf/rsavcaf9513.pdf.

200 **apparent failures of transparency under the law:** Jenna Johnson, "Federal Officials Probe Penn State for Possible Clery Act Violations," *Washington Post*, July 17, 2015; Lyndsey Layton, "Virginia Tech Pays Federal Fine for Failure to Warn Campus During 2007 Shooting Rampage," *Washington Post*, April 16, 2014.

200 **sexual assault on campus:** For a recent documentary about the issue, see *The Hunting Ground* (2015).

201 **almost none of what happens on campus:** The percent of crime reported to the FBI's Uniform Crime Report via the National Incident-Based Reporting System was 20 percent in 2004. "Forcible fondling" and "forcible rapes" were the fourth and sixth leading reported crimes from 2000 to 2004. See "Crime in Schools and Colleges," Uniform Crime Reporting, U.S. Department of Justice, FBI, https://ucr.fbi.gov/nibrs/crime-in-schools-and-colleges/crime_in_schools_and_colleges.

201 **maximum of expulsion:** Tyler Kingkade, "Fewer than One-Third of Campus Sexual Assault Cases Result in Expulsion," *Huffington Post*, September 29, 2014.

201 **Independent Police Review Authority:** "Second Quarter Report, April 1, 2016–June 30, 2016," City of Chicago Independent Police Review Authority, p. 3, http://www.iprachicago.org/2nd-quarter-report-2016/; Monica Davey and Timothy Williams, "Chicago Pays Millions but Punishes Few in Killings by Police," *New York Times*, December 17, 2015.

203 **extraordinary, withering, soulful:** Katie J. M. Baker, "Here's the Powerful Letter the Stanford Victim Read to Her Attacker," *BuzzFeed*, June 3, 2016.

206 **"Sitting in the sterile, antiseptic gray":** Mariame Kaba, Twitter post, June 7, 2016, https://twitter.com/prisonculture/status/74024386484 2317824.

207 **discretion of the judges:** Naomi Murakawa, *The First Civil Right: How Liberals Built Prison America* (New York: Oxford University Press, 2014), Kindle ed., pp. 10–11, 16, locs. 338–65, 459–70.

208 **White Americans are more likely:** Wesley Lowery, "More Whites Killed by Police, but Blacks 2.5 Times More Likely to Be Killed," *Chicago Tribune*, July 11, 2016.

208 **ratio of the incarceration rates:** "State-by-State Data," Sentencing Project, http://www.sentencingproject.org/the-facts/.

209 **"While heroin use has climbed":** Katharine Q. Seelye, "In Heroin Crisis, White Families Seek Gentler War on Drugs," *New York Times*, October 30, 2015.

210 **"no one came to me":** "Chris Christie's Plea to Change How America Handles Drug Addicts" (video), *Huffington Post*, November 4, 2015, https://www.youtube.com/watch?v=FdYMx7sycW4.

213 **radically reduced incarceration:** Lacino Hamilton, "Understanding the Human Cost of Imprisonment," *Truthout*, June 23, 2015.

213 **racial integration improves measurable outcomes:** David L. Kirp, "Integration Worked. Why Have We Rejected It?," *New York Times*, May 19, 2012.

214 **12 percent of the municipal revenue:** *Investigation of the Ferguson Police Department*, U.S. Department of Justice, Civil Rights Division, March 4, 2015, p. 14, fn. 12.

214 **prisons have become a central source:** Tracy Huling, "Building a Prison Economy in Rural America," in *Invisible Punishment: The Col-*

lateral Consequences of Mass Imprisonment, ed. Meda Chesney-Lind and Marc Mauer (New York: New Press, 2011).

214 **the $5 billion private prison industry:** Martha C. White, "Locked-In Profits: The U.S. Prison Industry, By the Numbers," *NBC News,* November 2, 2015.

SELECTED BIBLIOGRAPHY

Alexander, Michelle. *The New Jim Crow: Mass Incarceration in the Age of Colorblindness*. New York: New Press, 2012.

Andreas, Peter. *Smuggler Nation: How Illicit Trade Made America*. New York: Oxford University Press, 2014.

Bailyn, Bernard. *The Barbarous Years: The Peopling of British North America: The Conflict of Civilizations, 1600–1675*. New York: Vintage, 2012.

Balko, Radley. *Rise of the Warrior Cop: The Militarization of America's Police Forces*. Reprint edition. New York: PublicAffairs, 2013.

Biondi, Martha. *To Stand and Fight: The Struggle for Civil Rights in Postwar New York City*. Cambridge, Mass.: Harvard University Press, 2006.

Chesney-Lind, Meda, and Marc Mauer, eds. *Invisible Punishment: The Collateral Consequences of Mass Imprisonment*. New York: New Press, 2003.

Coates, Ta-Nehisi. *Between the World and Me*. New York: Spiegel & Grau, 2015.

Desmond, Matthew. *Evicted: Poverty and Profit in the American City*. New York: Crown, 2016.

Fanon, Frantz. *The Wretched of the Earth*. Translated by Richard Philcox. Reprint edition. New York: Grove Press, 2005.

———. *Black Skin, White Masks*. Translated by Richard Philcox. Revised edition. New York: Grove Press, 2008.

Fields, Karen E., and Barbara J. Fields. *Racecraft: The Soul of Inequality in American Life*. Reprint edition. London: Verso, 2014.

Forman, James. *Locking Up Our Own: Crime and Punishment in Black America*. New York: Farrar, Straus and Giroux, 2017.

Hirsch, Arnold R. *Making the Second Ghetto: Race and Housing in Chicago 1940–1960*. Chicago, Ill.: University of Chicago Press, 1998.

Jackson, Kenneth T. *Crabgrass Frontier: The Suburbanization of the United States*. New York: Oxford University Press, 1987.

Leovy, Jill. *Ghettoside: A True Story of Murder in America*. New York: Spiegel & Grau, 2015.

Murakawa, Naomi. *The First Civil Right: How Liberals Built Prison America*. New York: Oxford University Press, 2014.

Philbrick, Nathaniel. *Mayflower: A Story of Courage, Community, and War*. New York: Penguin Books, 2006.

Prince, Carl E. *The U.S. Customs Service: A Bicentennial History*. Washington, D.C: Dept. of the Treasury, U.S. Customs Service, 1989.

Self, Robert O. *American Babylon: Race and the Struggle for Postwar Oakland*. Princeton, N.J.: Princeton University Press, 2005.

Southern, Ed, ed. *The Jamestown Adventure: Accounts of the Virginia Colony, 1605–1614*. Winston-Salem, N.C.: John F. Blair, Publisher, 2011.

Stuntz, William J. *The Collapse of American Criminal Justice*. Cambridge, Mass.: Belknap Press of Harvard University Press, 2011.

Walvin, James. *A Short History of Slavery*. London: Penguin UK, 2007.

Whitman, James Q. *Harsh Justice: Criminal Punishment and the Widening Divide between America and Europe*. New York: Oxford University Press, 2005.

Wilkerson, Isabel. *The Warmth of Other Suns: The Epic Story of America's Great Migration*. New York: Vintage, 2010.

Zimring, Franklin E. *The Great American Crime Decline*. New York: Oxford University Press, 2008.

INDEX